20 Ways

—

To Heal

Transform your' thoughts and conditioned environments.   Create deeper satisfaction every day.

Michael Westin

OLD AGE Books©

New York, NY   Tokyo, Japan

Library of Congress Cataloging-in-Publication Data.

Westin, Michael.

Twenty Ways To Heal

OLD AGE Books©
New York, NY
www.twentywaystoheal.com

ISBN-10: 061-576-2115
ISBN-13: 978-061-576-2111
LCCN- 2013902221

Cover art work by Eric Santwire

DEDICATION

*This is dedicated to all those who never gave up
and held themselves to high standards,
so people Like us could have something more to give.*

3

Contents

5

Part 4:
HEALING ACTIONS
Expand Your' Feelings and Expand Your' life

Introduction

Twenty ways is a quick and easy guide that can create a direction on how to get beyond the status quo in your' own development. This is intended for getting peace, tranquility, satisfaction, grace and a healthy mindset in the worldly areas of work and general outside life. This book is about developing emotional intelligence and about how transforming thoughts and conditioned environments can create deeper satisfaction in everyday life and expand our own personal emotional palettes, in turn creating healing and a holistic mindset, therefore making the world a better place.

How come some people get through adversity with deep insightfulness and closeness, yet others just complain in the face of it? The difference is simple, if you focus on the adversity you attract and get more adversity. Yet, if you search out how to get through it, or how to make your' life better, you eventually will find answers and get results. And in all twenty ways in this book, an underlying pattern of conditioning yourself for positive manifestation is a present and repeated theme.

With a unique background of living in Asia for eight years, and at the same time having studied some of the best of the West's new forms of Psychology and personal development, make this book an interesting and perhaps even healing read for transforming habitual thoughts and conditioned environments.

This book is for the individual, not for social change in particular. It is written to be of usefulness for a CEO or a homeless person or for people who want to change something inside themselves. It's for true individual well being, a personal quality of feeling that you experience each day. If this book improves the quality of your' everyday life then it has accomplished its goal of being self healing.

Developing the subtle intuitions and insights, takes care and intricacy, as well as patience. This book will show twenty or more ways to transcend, start new, and have a new beginning, let go and heal the gross, hard, worldly habits of mind and thoughts. As well, as is written in a way that is insight-full of specific knowledge and places and gives many real life examples and creative solutions. Inside of each of the Twenty Ways, besides giving suggestions of specific things a person can do to be more in the "now" and "present", a pattern of language has been written and used that is a pattern inside of each of the specific healing ways. This pattern that constitutes "change" or "transformation" or what I call a "holistic mindset" can be called a "now" based approach to healing and transformation, in that time will be taken to create awareness of where we are putting focus and attention into our lives, right now, and how it is, that we are directing our own attention and focus.

Prologue

Everyone seems in such a bizzy these days, after all, weren't the modern handy devices supposed to make life easier? Well they will eventually and they will probably keep changing. Just as fast as we get used to them, the new ones will keep popping up. I just heard a talk today by a prominent Medical Doctor who said technology will be a billion times more advanced in ten years from now and we won't even be able to imagine what is going to happen.

So, there will be no status quo type of technology, this will be in a constant flux. The only thing that we can call status quo will be in our own development and experience, which hopefully won' t be "S.Q." anymore. What really effect's our own development? If you are fortunate enough to have grown up in a family or environment where you were able to manifest self sustainability, affluence and a healthful life for yourself and the people you care about, you probably care as to why nearly 50 percent of the people on earth live on less than two dollars a day and nearly 25 percent of people live on less than a dollar a day. Although, living in an attitude of gratitude is a healing method, we could probably agree it is never too early to expand on the positive. And here's a little preview about "gratitude." It is not enough to tell someone you are grateful, or write a note with merely words. This gratefulness spoken of here is an emotional feeling in your' body, something that can be seen on the face of someone. Now, I am not talking about training and teaching and reinforcing your' children with the "You Rock" attitude, which seemed to be the zenith of our culture, and the pinnacle achievement to be. Teaching people to feel like a rock star feels great. Yet a rock stars collective habits of mind and body seem to produce similar results. Which looking on their past behavior seem to leave predictable consequences such as, temper tantrums, self absorption, and destructiveness, just to name a few. I can rock, but I'm not talking about that. Such is life, when people delve into the deeper feeling of things and try

13

to share it out of love and passion. What other collective behaviors and habits have our cultural, music stars and their genres as well as society left us stuck with individually and as a whole through their propagation? Drugs are accepted as the answer for medical problems and are common treatment. It's okay to use foul language pretty much anywhere it seems like. It seems like the majority of people have been tricked or fooled into forgetting about one of the old golden rules. Happiness comes from the inside, not from money. Are you sucked into "The struggle for legal tender," as some of my friends say or are you "in the world but not of it?" Are you a person who thinks life was better back in the "good ol' days?" Do you think our society is getting better or worse? In this book we talk about twenty or so specific ways to make things new and transcend, none of which haven't been written about. And take a look at processes underlying our lives and how to affect those processes. In this book, the 20 or so healing ways account for about twenty percent of the power to heal, the other eighty percent is looking at internal processes. Understanding internal processes and influencing them is priority one here and that can be done through developing internal awareness and detachment. And recent breakthroughs in Psychology and personal development have shed new light on how our internal processes function.

This is meant to be an easy, thought provoking read. In turn, a trail can be left for your own personal tastes in your own future. Training yourself to alter your' own physiology consciously by doing such activities as celebrating is one of them. Not only celebrating the big things like birth days, weddings, and holidays, yet celebrating the little things can be rewarding on an emotional and physiological level. And that is one of the twenty ways to heal. Learning to influence your' own physiology with your' own volition in a natural way is broken down into learnable pieces in the upcoming chapters. Some sales training programs use celebration to create more sales. If you can close more deals by bringing more celebration into your' daily behavior, what else could you manifest more of by bringing other positive emotional states into your' life? In this book, awareness and utilization of positive emotional states of well being are used to enhance health, healing and wholeness. When we put positive energy out we attract like energies. How our thoughts effect our emotions, is one of the things you will be reminded of. And learning how to effect and take control of these processes in this book is explored here in a fun, simple and informative way. Celebrating is one of those habits.

Having grown up with some of the "Old World" tradition and conditioning makes me realize the past has attributes to be taught to present and future generations but we can't stay stuck in the past. If we keep thinking and putting the same energy out the same way we will get the same results. Which brings us to the question, what is healing?

1-What Is Healing?

Healing and health is very much the same thing. Generally, when people go to doctors, the doctor's traditionally will tell you that either you are sick or not. In other words they diagnose illness. If there is no disease or illness, treatment is not applied. After all, the medical model came from studying disease, finding what is wrong and eradicating and preventing the perceived causes of it. Hence, if there was nothing wrong treatment was not administered. And modern day psychology used the same process: study "mental illness" or dysfunction to find out how to overcome it. Modern medicine is very successful using this approach and has changed the world dramatically. Modern Medical Doctor's, even traditional one's more so than the past, may suggest ways to be healthy like one of my doctor's did by suggesting a book about how to be "younger next year." This kind of suggested reading from a "traditional" allopathic Medical Doctor can be described as a "Generative Change" technique in therapeutic and healing circles. Instead of just giving me pain pills, he is giving me more, in a whole new direction on many *different levels*. Thus the term "generative," meaning more than one thing is being effected setting off a multiple effect. He is beginning to instill the idea that there are other things that can actually, not only, take away the pain, but make you look and feel younger next year besides eliminating the ailment with pills or surgery. And perhaps, in turn, eliminate the problem all together while at the same time creating a larger life enhancement. Healing is about having wholeness, healthfulness, energy, and personal clarity. One simple definition of healing is being confident that your' life is on the right track, that you are doing all you can do with what you have given to you in the moment and having a satisfaction in life and a fearless attitude. This kind of mindset may add some healing energy to life. Many of the current day mental attitudes are based on old world ideas and methodologies, because our attitudes are a collection of our belief's and habitual thinking patterns. These can be obscure and hidden forms of emotional bondage and internal patterns that diminish life quality. Life is a joy to be lived and should be. Many of the ideas of today regarding mental health come from Freudian Psychotherapy. The idea that he gave us that a person can talk about their past and affect the present was cutting edge at that time over one hundred years ago. This was not a part of accepted behavior or tradition until then: making an appointment to speak to a doctor about your' past experiences to create a better life for oneself that is. Yet, now we know you can change your present not only by talking about the past, but by talking about the future too or many, many other ways. In fact, if you do anything different in your mind or body things are bound to change. It's doing the same things over and over again in the same way that keeps people "stuck." Adding awareness can really help. People seem to have gotten stuck on going into the past, and being stuck on the past is detrimental to going past things.

19

What if other industries used the medical model of inquiry and applied it to their field or business like much of modern day Psychology did? What if your sales organization took the worst performing salespeople and studied them as well as showcased them? They could hire several scientific people and document the worst persons behavior in fine detail, pinpointing with microscopic precision every word, action and misstep that the person made.   They could have the un-successful salesperson's case study published in "Salesperson Today" Magazine, telling people how to avoid turning into this person. And, they could have this person speak at every morning meeting, talking about their mistakes in total detail, perhaps in a really emotional way.   After all, adding emotion to things helps learning right?   Would this work in your' sales organization? No, it wouldn't fly probably. Why? People want to hear from the successful ones and they want to hear what works. The energy behind something is more important than the words. Eighty percent of success in transforming anything is Psychology, the other ten or twenty percent is mechanics and know how. In communication, studies have found that only seven percent of communication is actually the words, fifty percent is how the words are spoken or the voice tone. The same is true for our inside worlds and internal processes, it is not what we think, but *how* we think that is the difference that makes the difference. And this will be explored thoroughly here. If they took the best performers and top sales people and gave their accounts of their experience, their vibe would rub off on others more than any technique or scientific formula.

The relationship between your habitual thoughts and emotions and how they affect your physiology will not just be talked about here in Twenty Ways to Heal, but encouraged and integrated in your life. The words wholeness, holistic, health and healing are very closely related words. When your body and mind are synchronized you are healthy and/or at least moving in a healthy direction. When either your' body or mind are out of balance in a state of uneasiness or *dis*-ease, one needs healing or care and is not whole or healthy. The scale from being im-balanced to totally healthy can encompass many different levels and characteristics from thoughts and emotions

21

to biology and genetics. Twenty Ways to Heal deals more towards the emotional and psychological level than the physical level. Using your' current resources to expand and amplify your' emotions in a positive way can be transformative, healing and adds zest to life. If you have a physical problem or challenge, please see a certified doctor, and use this book to discover and have new thoughts and explore and find new questions in relation to having a healthy attitude and its effect on emotions, physiology and life balance. When people talk about relaxation, this just isn't getting a good massage from a masseuse. It is important not only for people to be able to learn how to release physical stress easily and effortlessly, but be able to develop their intuition to know which massage therapist is the right one to go to. You could make it a point to test several different massage styles. And there are other ways to relax without massage. So, Twenty Ways is more about subtle awareness and intuition. Otherwise, I could just give you the phone numbers and addresses of places to visit and all you would need to do is show up with an appointment and you're healed, full of clarity and the master of your mind. Of course, in this world we live in today, who knows what is really possible, seems like the sky is the limit.

This book is about your *interaction* in your experience of whatever your' experiencing, and about personal well being and clarity. Healing is using your' current inherent resources to amplify positive emotions in yourself, and generalize those emotional states into all areas of life in a systematic way. Knowing how to do that will be much clearer by the time you get toward the end of this book, if you put your full awareness in this and put a little effort into the simple exercises and creative visualizations.

2-The Twenty Ways

To Heal

In our experience of life, we all share common things and we all have an equal chance, in that we as human beings all share the same neurology and can pretty much have access to the same information anywhere in the world. Since we all share the same neurology, that means that we all have the same potential to influence our thoughts. And if we can change or influence our thoughts, we can change our feelings. When we change our thoughts and feelings then we can change our actions and our daily quality of life.

If you begin to wonder how you can make your life or the lives of others more healthful. It is important to realize that each person has a unique set of experiences that sets their lives apart from each other, as well as a part of each others. Just like we all have a unique finger print, so too do no two people share the same experiences. In this, our diversity as well as our individuality is emanated into our lives.

In order for one to heal, what has to happen? We have to be and come from that place of clarity and wisdom where we are in tune and in sync with the positive things in life. Be it action in the world or inactive solitude, in either place, one can experience a peace and clarity in any situation. When you bring a candle into a room the darkness disappears, the darkness does not need to be pushed away. The same is true in our minds or approaching any new endeavor. In order to change something, we have to learn from life and our mistakes and move on, without sinking in the muck or getting stuck or identified with the problem. The key is to learn and move on. Problems are temporary, we do not need permanent solutions to temporary problems. If you do something caring for someone else, this is healing. Once again, if you are having a life threatening problem, see a doctor. If you are currently seeing a doctor and are unhappy or think you can find someone better, perhaps you can change doctors. If you do not have the choice to change doctors, perhaps changing your' attitude can make the experience better, or trying anything different for that matter. Sometimes life just wants you to seek out something new. Just like the ocean, life has its peak waves, its calm days, stormy times and cold waters as well as it's warm swells. And once again, please don't make permanent solutions to temporary problems, and they are all temporary. If you watched the young man from Iraq who was left in a shoe box as a baby in the middle of a war zone singing "Imagine" on X-factor, then you realize that perhaps lots of stuff you thought wasn't small stuff is just that! Perhaps our biggest turmoil's are a call for us to make a change, seek it out and become more. In order to experience the deeper things in life someone has to be there to experience them. If you have no time or are preoccupied with your day, the past or future or whatsoever, then the oneness, connection and flow with life is diminished. And yes, it is possible to be totally busy and still have balance and a relaxed mindset in spite of worldly endeavor, you do not need to go and sit in a cave in the Himalaya's for five years to have this.

It is as if you are trying to watch a movie and someone is having a popcorn fight in the cinema. Yes, you could probably tell me what happened there in the movie, yet your experience of it was unfulfilling. Such is life, if our own emotions and thoughts are covered or cluttered. And living with voracious resolve and emotion can be achievable for anyone as well as passing it on to others. We need to develop rituals and habits to create more enhanced states of mind and emotion.

These twenty 'healing' methods are nothing but enhancing our mind and emotions on different levels. Some of them can just be read and forgotten about. Perhaps some night when you are out with friends perhaps you will remember some little thing that will continue to expand the clarity and connectedness you are feeling that you did not remember until then. It could be something someone said to you or that you shared with another. Or some other healing ways have specific exercises that will make the book act like an interactive guide where you can compare your own personal input or internal thoughts, written or not written, within a unique healing pattern, patterns or paradigm. Most of the techniques are subjective. And that is one of the problems in life, and people seem to be making lots of hassle and fights over subjective stuff. One thing about subjectivity is that you can't put your finger on it. It's just like the general tendencies of emotions or feelings. This process that is done a few times here is capable of in and of itself heightened states of awareness.

Just like people make internal awareness states in preparation for just about everything, be it tests, concerts, intimacy, sightseeing, learning (sadly it seems many schools seem to think that being in a good mood is not conducive to learning) or competing in sports.

In fact some of the most exquisite things in life require and have come from people who have highly developed internal sensory apparatus. Some of the best inventions that have changed the course of humanity have come from people well known to have gone inside themselves in dream like states and come back with the ideas for electricity and for the Theory of Relativity. Now artists, musicians, writers as well as poets often describe the feeling of being taken over and something coming over them. Even the wealthiest people throughout history have purchased the best art, hired the best musicians and read the best books. These works of art carry a uniqueness and expression that are so individual and unique that their value is invaluable. So somewhere even the subjective things in life have their pinnacle. The ways to heal described in this book are mostly subjective and they are some of the most subjective things in life. They are less about achievement and more about how to enjoy doing nothing at all or enjoying your' free time. Yet, they can enhance the mundane things such as repetitive things at work or difficult situations. They are more about serendipity and less about planning. And lastly, The Healing

Patterns are about enjoying what you already have, and not striving to get something. And when a person can be totally content with what they have, a clarity will arise within' and make it easier to attract and manifest whatever you truly want. And if you are already totally successful in worldly terms and are searching for a deeper meaning or insight, great! And if you are still trying to make it in the world, and looking for a deeper meaning or insight, also great! Once you have this clarity, the pathway gets a little brighter and easier. On that note: let's get a little objective about subjectivity.

3-Objective Subjectivity

One of the challenges of dealing with things of this nature is that, who wants to go into feelings? As a culture, some people really frown upon this. That is the cool thing about "Objective Subjectivity," because it is possible to share stuff without the content. You may ask, "What do you mean share feelings without content?" This can be done when people take some kind of inventories of their own or other people's emotions, which could be in any context, like a work context, or let's say for example a personal emotion list. You can do this without the subjective interpretations if you choose. This is as much of a tool for the trainer, practitioner or manager as it is for the listener, attendee, or counseled who may not want to give up personal information or be misinterpreted or misunderstood by the unpredictability of language, especially regarding emotions. This is done by effective communicators all the time.

The same process can be used in the transformation of habitual thoughts. Recognizing that the thinking process has an effect on emotions and vice-versa, these two areas, thoughts and emotions are where we will explore. Some people may be afraid that if they get into too much feeling stuff that they lose control. This may cause them to look stupid or perform badly in front of others or in a professional situation. That's true! That's maybe why children are more in tune emotionally than most adults because they haven't shut them down yet nor are they judged as much by them. But we are not going to do that here. When we think in new ways we feel differently. When we feel differently, we have different thoughts that can create different actions and patterns. When we have new thoughts and actions we get new results. Do feelings or thoughts precede action, or vice-versa? Whatever way is more prevalent or true, I think we could agree that they are closely related. Our perceptions of time and of the past and the future, as well as how this relates to our current well being is an interesting and important piece of 20 ways of healing.

The best thing about the past is that *it is past.* The small little things that we make internal habits of can create and expand positive states of well being. Something that is relaxing for you like a calming favorite song or whichever one, can even increase, stabilize and balance this in the directions that only you can choose now, because it is your' subjectivity, feeling and thought. Getting to share good feelings is one thing, creating rituals and building, growing and fine tuning our own personal enhancement is a never ending and constant process that continually grows and can have an automation that is easy and effortless over time.

One problem with language and words is that the semantic relations of the words used by different people in the world have their own personal histories. They can go either or any way. So many times, our words do not connect, even the words we use to describe our own emotions. If you say "I'm stuffed," in N. America, it means something totally different than in the U.K. And this type of comparison is even finer and subtler when dealing on an emotional level between two people, in relationships, personal development and expressing emotions or even ideas for that matter. Sometime, instead of calling an emotion by its name, do an experiment of just calling them by a letter like 'A, B or C." Keep watching them, labeling them with letters, you will find that this is a fun little experiment that generates interesting awareness of how the words we use to attach meaning to our emotions and feelings can effect and influence them apart from the feelings themselves.

Learning and experimenting with your' own internal subjectivity and being objective about it will do two things. First, it will take away some of the confusion that the ambiguities of language inherently carry with them by not labeling the feeling or emotion with specific words. And second, it will begin a new awareness of the underlying pattern of internal feeling states and internal processes. Awareness is one of the "Gem" attributes that develops over time and effects multiple areas of behavior and emotion. Emotions and feelings have patterns and characteristics, just like certain colors of a painting have characteristics. Lighter colors are lighter and darker colors are heavier usually. As you start to notice the *locations* and *movements* of emotions, over time, you will notice certain patterns of where you feel the emotions in the body, and the directions and movement of emotions. Direction, location and movement are the "objective" part of the "subjective" experience. Where in the body is the emotion located and what direction is it moving in? This attention to awareness over time is a revealing habit in that you will be surprised when some feeling that you had experienced, for perhaps a long time, suddenly reveals itself to you. And you realize that all the words and drama that you had done, in analyzing and attaching words to it may seem like a joke, in perspective of a new emotional intelligence and awareness. And you can build whatever emotions inside yourself that you choose over time easily. We will go into this in more detail throughout the book. Just like a fine connoisseur of wine develops that sensual sensitivity for smell and taste and can tell you what it is without even seeing the bottle. So it is true of our emotions, as your' feelings develop in new ways and you begin to notice objective patterns of movement, location, and pulses of feelings and can expand and let these grow in new ways that bring new ways of feeling and more choices in life. And as you do this not only will you get to feel and share more emotion, but your' emotional muscle will develop and you won't be at the mercy of your' emotions as much as you used to be.

4-Let go of the past-Here's how!

Everybody has heard and knows that they should let go of the past. Has anyone ever told you "don't live in the past?" Did that help you to not live in the past and let go? And has anyone ever really told you "how?" Now, if I told you to quit dwelling on the past, that is a little different from saying let go of the past. Our habitual way of regurgitating past experiences sometimes emboldens them just out of sheer habit, and letting go of this grip sometimes just needs motivation or a pure concise and solid decision. Now, I want to make it clear that remembering and dwelling on positive resources from the past is and can be healing, but that is not what this chapter is about.

One catch phrase recently is be here in the now, and people will sometimes get angry at you if they feel like you are distracting them from being in their own "Now" space, like you have to fight for your' right to be in the present. When really they are just saying, "I believe being in the 'now' is important." Or. that they think they are on a higher level then you are because they are more in the now then the other person, how funny! Perhaps some are not skilled enough to maintain their own serenity of mind in the face of distraction and need constant aloofness to function. With experience and awareness one can learn to maintain these deeper states in more places easily and effortlessly. The skill of being able to stop your' mind of any internal talk and be totally in the present moment in spite of anything else that is going on is very useful to do. Meditating or doing self hypnosis is useful for calming the mind and creating in the "moment-ness" and the habit of letting go of unwanted thoughts and feelings. Exercise, travel, walking or many other things can be similar. Look what happened to all those people who were doing this in the Sixties, they kind of got stuck in that moment and some of them are still stuck "in that moment." So, people need to be able to be in the moment at any time and still at other times or together be able to focus on what they want and on a direction in which they are moving in or would like to go.

If you are living in the past and dwelling on the old disempowering events or memories, whatever they are, than you are just stuck in old feelings and habitual memories that make a person incapable of even seeing what is happening in this moment. That is the biggest loss. That is, being caught up in the past and not being attune to what is happening right now. If a person can realize that they are losing more and getting worse feelings by not being able to see and be aware of what is happening right now, then they may let go of it. This is not to say that, things that have happened in the past are not being presented to us because they one hundred percent categorically have nothing to say or show to us or are worthless.

Sometimes things such as memories or feelings come up, perhaps even ones we have not remembered previously. Sometimes these need serious consideration and the help of a doctor or therapist. If your therapist does not make you feel at least a little better in one session, maybe you can find a better one. There are many people who can get good results in one session. Also, if someone is forcing you to go back into the old traumatic memories, or pressuring you to relive them, or pressuring you to talk about them, get a new person to talk to, especially if they had trauma of any kind in the memory. Just talking and reliving past junk and bad memories to "unclog" the pain or "let out" the built up unexpressed emotion like it is molasses or something, sometimes just makes them worse and more manifested in the present. If a person gets sick of talking about them that is when change can happen. Getting clear on what you want instead, gives a direction to go into, focus on that. The same questions used in the compelling future's chapter can be applied to our emotional states and feelings or anything for that matter.

What you put your' attention and awareness on manifests and grows. If you just need someone to talk to, make it a point to try and give energy to what you really want or explore that more, instead of wallowing in the muck too much or repeatedly!

Sometimes people just need to talk to someone and that is fine. But don't become identified too much with the problem or pain. And remember, you are not your' problems, but much larger than anything that could ever happen to you. This is the ultimate time to be involved in self exploration and healing. And you can flip to the "Scramble it Pattern," in chapter twelve, for changing unwanted, uncomfortable or traumatic memories and feelings literally instantly.

One of the things I learned from a teacher in Hawaii is that when problems come up, past negative memories that is, we need to be able to learn from these, yet not get stuck in them. If you suppress them, you miss out on an opportunity to get what these messages or memories are trying to relay to a person. If you just try to 'let go" of these types of memories by pushing them away, you miss out on the chance to get the learning's from them. Most times we do not even have to get the learning's but just stop dwelling on stuff. A cool way to explore these messages, especially if they keep coming up is to do a light hearted visualization. This is intended to be a fun exercise used as a general background or idea of the paradigms of "let go." And getting in tune with the messages and the learning's life is giving us, so we can learn from the mistakes and the circumstances of life can be interesting and revealing. People do not need to do this kind of visualization to learn or transcend or let go. Yet this can be useful, sometimes interesting things present themselves and it also can be relaxing. If you have someone else to read this to you or you can just say it in a slow and soothing voice some time, or after reading it and getting the gist of the process, it can be read or imagined or spoken inside for yourself all alone. (*New Meaning Visualization*)

In a quiet setting where you will not be disturbed, if you need to tell someone you need quiet time, or to put a do not disturb sign, or "Please respect going Into THE ZONE" sign on the door do it. Just sit or lay down in a relaxed fashion and, feel your body there, be comfortable and let any sounds direct you inside even more. And ask yourself, "what experience or feeling can I begin to let go of now that by getting a deeper understanding of it can create a new and free space to begin to create a new enhanced feeling or direction or emotion in my life?"

Just float up and outside yourself, seeing yourself from above, just as if you are an outsider watching yourself from above...just relaxing where ever you happen to be. Imagine you are in a protective bubble floating above yourself, easily and in a comfortable way now. Floating above in that protective bubble now...just after the original or first occurrence of that unwanted or needed experience or emotion now, that once the message is understood it can begin to change into something new. Easily and effortlessly still relaxing...there...once you get the message it is trying to give, you can begin letting go of that. Now comfortably and gently ask, "What is the message I need to learn from this now so that I can let go of it now?" Staying comfortably floating there, being patient for an answer in the form of words,

43

thoughts or feelings. When you have a clear answer, in the form of a new insight or perhaps it's a new action that you need to begin doing in your' life, you can move on now. Or perhaps it's to drop something that doesn't serve you or to take an action that serves yourself better and your highest needs better. Once you have that new insight or message now, start the last step of going in time to just before the very first memory or experience of the original occurrence of what you don't want any more now. Being just before this experience, in time now, take a few moments, being just before that original experience there in that safe space, float down before that old event, all the way down just before that old event happened. And start walking in time through the actual event, in that protective bubble, see that in a new way, and hear that in a new way. And notice, that the feeling is different now, isn't it? All the learning's can stay with you and you keep going through all those experiences, and towards now. In this secure feeling, making your way, all the way back now. Preserving all of the learning's and noticing yourself in similar situations in the future, acting in nothing but new ways, in similar experiences now. Taking as much time as you need too, and feeling relaxed, at the end of the exercise.

After taking a few minutes to come all the way back from this "let go" exercise, open your eyes, you may take the "going into the zone" sign down as a necessary part of your' personal relaxing ritual if you like to call it that.

One other way to let go is to learn about time lines. Time lines are how the sub conscious part of a person sorts our past thoughts and future hopes or dreams. You can probably have a thought of the next big holiday or event that you could be celebrating, and notice its location in space. If you think about past memories, notice the location of the memories over a continuum or progression of years. If you find yourself thinking about memories from the past yet making the size and images of them larger than they should be, make the images small,

45

very small and put them into the past where they belong...the smaller and further away the better...even becoming smaller that a speck of dust sometimes. Most times you don't even need to "seek out" the hidden messages, just pushing away or minimizing the thoughts is enough, just making them the size of a little speck of dust that in the end just blows away, never to be seen nor heard of again now!

Having problems is part of being human. So, all the problems started because we were born maybe. I am not sure if there is anyone who is totally clear and problem free. But I have met many people who have had lots of problems and act like they don't have a care in the world, yet are still caring and successful. Sometimes to let go, a person just needs to decide to, or get fed up with it all and just stop thinking about them and just do something else. Be it thinking of something in a new way or doing something physical. And trying to do it with awareness and learning to do things in new ways can really happen in an easy way.

Talking about the past as a way to try to have a better life seems to be very common these days. The idea that you could talk about life events and change the present, at one time did not exist. People associate intelligence with analyzing the deep causes of a person's current behavior, when actually they limit the chances for future change and transformation by seeking the causes. Even though they may be "right," they really are not intelligent because they do not know the skills of transformation and are stuck on causes! Freudian Therapy and free association introduced this idea a long time ago and it changed everything all over the world. This was only available to the elite folks who could afford to go to therapy for five years, and pay someone to listen to them for all that time. These days people in general are more affluent, but they are looking for faster results and change as well as self sufficiency and independence and doing it on their own. Letting go of the past is one of the twenty ways to heal because it seems like one of the things people dwell on too much that gives so little solace or result. But also it is included here because it seems like one of the most prevalent, and therefore one of the rustiest, gross and grimy things that people habitually regurgitate that keeps them stuck. Sometimes people just need to say "stop," and ask themselves, "what else can I focus on that would be life enhancing or beneficial to me?" Perhaps something you are grateful for, or something you are about to work on that drives you. Or perhaps even go into the zone and meditate, anything would be better that regurgitating old funky junk. There are even some forms of healing or therapy that only work with new thoughts and behaviors, believing that giving the past impetus only strengthens the past. On a behavioral level it's true. When you indulge in a behavior, the neural networks are reinforced and strengthened each time!! When you remember things or habitually think about stuff, those same networks are reinforced. When we consciously recondition our thoughts, we can change our lives and even our daily quality of feeling and emotional states of being. This can be done with precision, articulateness and conscientiousness.

If you feel or think that you need to let go of the past, it begins with a conscious decision and realization that your life can be better by deciding to notice what you want that you enjoy or could enhance your' life, and striving for that. You can just start to catch yourself in the right times or the "wrong" times depending on how you look at it...and just stop it and do something new...anything!! Seek out advice from others who would like to accentuate your skills and accentuate positive emotions. Most people are better at minimizing good feelings than they are at amplifying good feelings. And it is not only you doing this to yourself. If you are going to learn from the past, get the learning's from it, learn from past mistakes, and then get the heck out of there. Your past can be used as a tool, use it, break it into pieces, perhaps even make a kaleidoscope of it. And make sure you use it to your advantage.

5-Get Away For a While

Ah, what better activity or inactivity could one do besides get away for a while? Whether being active or mellow while away, or perhaps even mellow active, getting away has obvious advantages and some subtler or more particular merits. One of which is being in a *new environment.* The well known Psychologist, B.F. Skinner, believed that *Environment* is the predominating factor that shapes behavior. Whether or not you believe it is a predominating factor for people, I'm sure you can agree that the place where we spend most of our time carries gravity and is very important.

So how can changing environments be healing? Usually the things that keep us stuck are reinforced by not only our own internal processes, but by external reinforcements or stimuli. Getting away for a while gives a person a chance to not be at the mercy of hidden or more obvious pulls and triggers. I would guess most people have had the experience of being in a really good mood and just sailing along on your day and some outside external trigger happens that reminds you of something else unrelated, and suddenly the wind is taken out of your' sails. This could be in the form of a phone call, e-mail, a traffic incident, listening to the radio, TV, a personal relationship or even something simple like an innocent statement from a co-worker or a word from someone who had no bad intention, that just inadvertently triggered some response. But besides these obvious stimuli or happenings, the buildings, roads, people, music, land and place we live in can carry "reinforcer's" and weight. "Reinforcer's" are external or internal stimuli that are conditioned and associated or paired with certain feeling states and behavior and they carry weight sometimes at a very subtle level. Will getting away take away all of these triggers? No, yet it can reduce and diminish them significantly. But reducing these is not the only advantage of getting away, making new decisions is, kind of like taking time to sleep on something before making a decision. And with a little foresight and planning, you can even reduce these external stimuli even more. And when you arrive back, hopefully your enhanced awareness and clarity will inoculate the old patterns or enhance them in new ways. Plus, our emotional feeling states of being are usually attached and connected to the places we spend the most time in. Just by getting to new environments, new chances can be presented to create and instill fresh beginnings, endings, feelings, and thoughts in an easy and effortless way even. And remember, usually people's stressors don't change, but people change on the inside. You usually cannot control the external stressors and stimuli, but you can change your' response to them.

This is not just about getting away from gadgets. Although, I am sure you would agree that would be helpful for certain reasons. So much of our lives are surrounded by phones and computers, it is as if people only have a minute or so attention span. When my generation was growing up they said that we only had about a 15 minute or so attention span, as that was how often commercials breaks came on TV. Now a days, I am not sure if people even have a one minute attention span...perhaps only a 5 or 10 second span at most. When the next stimuli or thing catches us, our attention and direction changes to that and it is acceptable and normal to do that. Psychologists say the reason that kids get so addicted is that they are able to get 30-50 reinforcer's per minute. That is, they get a gamut of feelings in one minute which are paired and conditioned inside and along music and visual actions scenes in the games. Where else can a person get so many and so much stimuli? And when a kid starts playing games at a very young age, don't you think they are easy customers to get hooked? After all, all those new graphics, sounds and triggers are interesting to kids, just like most everything else new is to them. And they get associated to the actions of playing the games and those actions, sounds and images become triggers for positive feelings to them.

So, where to get away to? You can get away in your' own home if you do it correctly. And when you come back to your regular world, you will know something has changed when the same trigger, reinforcer or stimuli happens and the response has changed, flattened or diminished. Or if triggers are not a factor for you, you may just notice a better peace of mind in most areas. And even after getting away, if you come back and the old patterns or triggers seem to happen again, that's okay! Because getting away and relaxing along with conscious effort is good for the mind and body anyways. And if you can go to someplace that you have not been before, even if in the same town your' living in, that is even better, especially if you are trying to heal something in particular. Does it make it better if it's even farther away? No! The distance is not as important as getting out of the conditioned environments and the conscious awareness and understanding these types of ideas bring. And if you have a family, you can surely give them the gift of taking a break too. If the family does not want to come, you can kindly tell them what time you will call as to not have to deal with surprises, or you could ask them to text if there is an emergency.

And a day or two can be enough time. Now you do not need to go out and climb some mountain as some people like to do. Impressing the neighbors or yourself and co-workers by climbing Mt. Fuji on the weekend is not what getting away as a healing method is about. Getting away from and trying to generate awareness is what this is about. And if you can develop and generate some of your' own internal triggers or reinforcements that are stronger in an emotional sense than any outside trigger or stimuli, the stronger one will collapse the other one's automatically and generative change will begin growing and manifesting. The "stronger" one is usually measured by emotional depth and intensity.

Giving yourself space and connecting with your' own self is what this is about. If you can do that by climbing Fuji San, or by running a marathon, great! Recognizing that there is a difference between our everyday conditioned environment and conscious environmental creation, while being aware of them is the utmost key here. And choosing the times and places and having recognition of the times when you will deal with them gives you more choice and flexibility. If you want to be involved in something competitive and throw out some energy and intensity and cathart, that is a different thing then just getting away for a while.

If you live in a city, perhaps going somewhere quiet with clean air and few people for a night or two will be nourishing. And if you live in a small town maybe going to a city where no one knows you and having a meal at a nice café or restaurant would be invigorating and wholesome. When you come back, make note of a few insights or learning's you have gained and apply them into your' usual life schedule and you may find a few subtle changes have taken root into the mundane or gross and repetitive areas even. Getting away for a while isn't a new idea. I have heard even great Masters like Jesus used to get away from the world and go to the mountains or deserts just to get away. I have heard that Lao Tzu, the Chinese Master, used to go for long walks, telling people beforehand that he did not want to be talked to, nor wanted to speak to anyone during the walk. And if you go somewhere that you really find stays with you, even when your' back to where you came from, great! Then, you can go back, again, to where you went the first time.

If not, you can find somewhere new to go once again. And after you find a "get away" that makes life better that you keep going to. You just might discover, you may eventually even learn how to "get away" without even going anywhere.

6-The third way to Heal-Cleanse

Cleansing is a really good way to immerse and expedite change to the bodies energy levels and get rid of stuff (toxins) from your body in a concise, focused period. One of the great things about a cleanse is that you can do it for as little as a few days and you either get a result or not. The end result is felt in better clarity, energy levels and all around well being. One key is to use your body's own healing mechanisms and enhance these and amplify them. Whereas, so many health plans promise a result, perhaps in a few months and sometimes the results are questionably lacking or hard to pin point. Now, a cleanse is not intended to lose weight particularly, yet to enhance health. With a good cleanse, usually you will get a result if you are doing it right. And if you have the opportunity to take a dark field look at your live white blood cells before and after the cleanse, you not only will feel the difference before and after the cleanse, but you can see the difference as the cells will look different and more whole and healthy.

If you are unfamiliar with cleansing, it is taking a few days or longer and deliberately eliminating the built up toxins that have accumulated in the body. This is done by having a special intake of live, fresh foods and sometimes supplements or herbal remedies. Many times a mental or psychological aspect is added along with the physical intake to help calm the mind and enhance the cleanse even more. This can be, listening to relaxing music, chanting, prayer, sound healing or using sound to enhance subtle energies. Many times additional physical movement in the form of stretching or walking is encouraged as this can oxygenate the body and enhance circulation and help the cleanse. Working with breath and doing some sort of breath work is common. Massage is commonly offered or included as a relaxation and healing enhancement as well.

You can do these kind of cleanses on your' own. I would recommend doing one with a skilled person first. Even if you are feeling good many people like doing a cleanse and perhaps do these every so often. You can take what you have learned from your' first cleanse and do it on your own the next time if you so choose or need to. Or you may want to do it with others at the same time. It is pretty easy to find a good place to do a cleanse these days. Usually, you will feel so good after a cleanse, that you will automatically generate new habits of healthfulness, without disciplined action, and you will find yourself going back to doing periodic cleanses without strict planning. Also, you may find yourself making new decisions during these times of clarity, perhaps even life changing decisions. What better place to make decisions? Yes, if you find yourself making bad decisions in unclear times of your' life, don't do that. Do a cleanse first, then in that new internal clarity space, make a new decision. I guarantee you, this type of decision will be more creative and true. When your body is in balance and you are in tune with your' higher needs, it is easier to feel certain and confident in your' new and true decisions. If you can do a cleanse with a Natural Health Care Practitioner, that would be the best. As these kind of things are really what they do for a living. Also, Ayurvedic cleanses are very good and there are many places to do them. Henna, Ayurveda, Tantra, Meditation as well as Yoga all come from India, one of the oldest cultures and these are usually offered at most places that offer Ayurveda. There are many places in S. India in the state of Kerala. The Chari Center of Health, in Santa Barbara, is a good guide for cleansing and healing.

Another good place to do a cleanse is on Koh Phangan island in the Sea of Thailand. The place is called Orion and Moti runs a real pretty place with all kinds of healing stuff including a steam bath and it's right on the water. Going to the island in and of itself is relaxing and healing as the air is clean, it's quiet, and the locals are friendly and just happy for no reason it seems. Even if you live in N. America or Europe you may consider it, as costs are quite different there because of exchange rates and that can offset the travel expense or eliminate it. And you can incorporate this into an extended vacation. I would highly recommend checking this place out if you are considering doing a cleanse. They have a world famous full moon party on the island, so I would book in advance, and you may not want to be there on the full moon or during busy season as many tourist types and party types are there. Yet, some people like the party and there is usually very good music. And the beach has a sunset and a sunrise side, so you can watch the sunset, then the full moon, dance all night long and see the sunrise if you like. Of course there is plenty of opportunity to dance every night there, not just full moon night. I noticed quite a few families coming there now, and they have a yoga retreat center on island now. Doing this, you could cover many of the 20 ways to heal in one shot. You can get away, dance, cleanse and...

7-Go The Opposite Way

Someone told me once, "look at what the masses are doing and do the opposite, you will probably have a better chance." This chapter could be called, "Do what works!" In other words, don't do what you think works as an action to make a difference in your life, just because everyone else is saying it or you see it in the media. An exquisite life takes mastery and discipline and you can't get that from reading headlines. Yet, the irony of this is that an exquisite life really is simple fundamentally. And by exquisite, I am talking about people who have a lot of freedom and many choices to chose from as well as directions to take in life if they like.

So, the biggest thing here is doing something at the minimum that allows a gage to be placed that measures direction!! Even if you are running the opposite way, that is fantastic in more than one way because at least you are committed to a better life, which sometimes just takes a little motivation. And, you are at least paying attention to general tendencies of culture and acting in some way...perhaps the opposite. The secondary attributes of doing the opposite or paying attention to culture is that your sensitivity develops with awareness. Also, you start to gage your' actions based upon what works, not on what people tell you or on your beliefs. Beliefs are what keep people stuck, yet they are the anchors or solidity that can get us through the muck or even to fly to new heights as well as do exquisite things. The certainty people feel inside themselves is a double edged sword, it gives us definiteness of feeling, yet this definiteness of feeling closes minds to new ideas or opportunities sometimes. The collective habits of many cultures is exemplified in media, you can see it everywhere. Some of these exemplifications of culture carry a life of their own, creating a sub-culture or even art, such as dance culture or the car culture that was popular in the 50's and still is today. Smoking used to be a popular sub-culture, everyone was doing it practically, now it isn't so much, but you can go to Hooka Bars in many places nowadays. This is commonly accepted culture among most, smoking flavored tobacco out of big colorful tubular bongs.

So, whether you go against the flow, or go with the flow, if you recognize which way the flow is going, you can, with awareness, have an edge up on your' own life and decisions compared to most others who are just caught up in the game, flow, rat race, collective unconscious, struggle for legal tender, or whatever you want to call it. You do not really need to "go the other way," but just notice which way the flow is going or the direction. And having awareness about your' own life and patterns as well as a pulse on the social level can create balance and directedness. Which brings the next thing...

Chapter 8-Dance For No Reason

This way to heal is fantastic. If you watch dancers that is even fantastic. Where does the unquestioned magnificence come from? Well, I can't answer that one hundred percent but who cares. It just is...and some things can't be explained nor should they be over analyzed or explained.

Since dancing is so physical, perhaps that is why it is so fantastic. What would you rather watch, an attractive dancer or an attractive weight lifter. Although both may exemplify the perfection of the human body, dancing has more rhythm and is more dynamic. But dancing is integrative. Aside from an aerobic benefit, this wonderful activity can be balancing to not only the body but to the mind and emotions.

Getting into a creative flow state through dancing can be very healthy. Where else can you go and forget about your problems, and alter your physical movements and breathing patterns, without any judgment, thinking or preplanned goal or outcome. And even understanding why dancing is integrative can be useful and beneficial. If you are older, please don't shut out this idea. When our eighty something year old friend Sam arrived at the dance club dressed real nice and seeming real cheerful, you can't believe how it made us feel. We need you. You wouldn't believe how you can affect us! And he is really just enjoying himself. And dancing is a good way to go with the breeze, be carefree and let your body take you away with the music. Free floating into good times, rhythms and feelings for no reason at all.

The good news is, once you know how to easily approach this and where to do this, you can always go back to it, even if you are "problemed" or "unproblemed" in the moment, it will always be there for you. And who knows, it may even "un-problem" you for a little while or you may spontaneously forget to have your problems. You can dance to many different kinds of music, as most people have many different musical tastes. The dance may be done differently depending on your mood and the music. And there are probably nearly as many different musical styles as there are dances. Some friends of mine used to have dance parties in the forests of Portugal and Goa, as they believed dancing was sacred and the quietness and environment of the trees carried a hidden healing power that they felt could be shared even after the party was over. Even though it was a business for them, the dancing was designed to be captivating and transforming, as it was.

Do this alone as an experiment, in your' room, living room, on the balcony or deck, or in even the kitchen for that matter. Cover your eyes, or don't try to notice how your movement is...forget about noticing yourself or how your performance looks...totally. Put the song on that you love or have a good feeling for, perhaps one that is soothing or uplifting. When the music starts, don't think, stop all internal talk, look down inside, feel your' body and let your body flow....easily and smoothly and just be quiet on the inside. Make the dancing a going in...not an outgoing thing. Remember, make this dancing an inward thing and journey...let your' body take you at the start...let your body move you. Slowly, slowly you can put more expression to it over time. You may spin around, wave your arms, just you and no one else, as if you are talking without words or, you are making a picture without a canvas or paper. Make the first few minutes of each dance an inward meditation or prayer, then slowly bring those feeling's out and express them, letting your' body sort of take you away.

I find this "going in" approach to dancing as something that gets developed more and more over time. It is also something you can do all on your' own and helps you to connect with a deeper part of yourself. If you are single this may seem more convenient to do, yet couples and women really love this. Women in general seem to be more in tune with their bodies, at least on a subtle or deeper level. Yet, this can be very transforming for a guy. It seems like the only way people have to express themselves these days is through written or visual media e.g. watching TV, reading books or playing sports. I guarantee you, if you go out dancing for 2 or 3 hours like this, you will leave feeling better than you did at the start, having more energy, alertness and vitality.

Now, this is not the kind of thing you can enjoy at a typical night club or bar. These types of places breed too much of the gazing crowd and lots of people are trying to compete to be the best dancer and so on. Most dance clubs I've been to are easy places to be able to be alone and not bothered by others. You can try to look for trance, house music, disco, techno, or 80's dance. And some places have more meditative dance styles or Sufi Dancing or whirling. It may not be easy to find a good place. A good DJ is usually very experienced at bringing the crowd "up," and they have a whole separate culture. Some of the best and light hearted dance music is 80's, and it is available easily everywhere and most of it is good quality. If you don't think you can go to a club in your area and want to make your' own dance parties, I would highly suggest going to any record store and getting a few 80's dance or disco CD's.

They are clear of profanity and have high quality production and instrumentation, as well as musicianship and lyrics.

As far as dancing with others, I usually always dance with others. I used to live in a small town that had their own community of dance get togethers. One guy I know changed towns and states in part just to be able to be a part of the occasional dances they would have. Yet, if you are going to really express the meeting of male and female energies in Salsa or Tango, that is considered a different thing than a way to heal or the dancing talked about here, even though it is healing.

So, just letting your body go with the music is considered one way to heal. You can start by yourself alone in a room perhaps in the day or night time, you may even add some candlelight to this. If you go out once a week for a few hours of dancing and can really find others to go out with who like to dance alone great, that's the best. This is definitely more of a common cultural thing in Europe, and some people think it is even funny to write about it in a book because it is so prevalent to them. Because they have a lot more dance "clubs" there. And perhaps one day some song will come on somewhere and without a plan or schedule a dance happens in you and you just feel so happy. I have never been anywhere where people always dance alone. But it should be a place where there is no pressure to dance with another or where you feel like you have to ask someone to dance. Plus, this can be something to look forward to every week. If you dance at home alone a few times here and there, this pure fun may be something you go back to with new music from time to time and can enjoy with other friends into the future. This can be an opportunity to listen to new music as well as something that grows and is integrative over time.

One of my favorite dancers is eighty four years old. If the energy is not right, he leaves. He not only seems to be very joyous dancing alone sometimes, yet has no problem dancing with others. His lady friend, who's around the same age, who is not able to stand up for very long, comes to the dance floor and stands up a few times here and there and dances so softly until she can't anymore than rests. Then gets up for a little bit again, and then rests. When talking with her, I could tell that she just loves expressing herself and sees dancing as a great way to not only express herself, but to connect with yourself and others, perhaps on a deeper level, beyond words. So, if you are gruff or sweet, young or old, rich or poor, want to move like Bruce Springsteen or even a Tai Chi Artist, can't speak the language, are missing a leg or even two, then look down inside, feel your emotions and body, feel & hear the music, and move your' body and enjoy!

9-Precision Direction Enhancement-

Compelling Futures

This is called "precision direction" because most people have set some direction in their lives such as, going to get education, savings plans, and health goals. But with precision direction setting, you can gain the benefits of the inherent traits of attraction and manifestation but with advanced internal representations of feeling goals, which are capable of setting new directions on subtle levels. You can make your' future something to entice and allure you. And knowing how to feel good for no reason can even inoculate past problems and tendencies. This brings setting goals to a new category of feeling goals or emotional state enhancement goals called "now" goals coupled with larger so called "big picture" thing goals, such as a new house or contributing something to a children's home or to be part of a positive change.

The goal is the same here for everyone. That is to feel fantastic every day, in spite of even physical pain or challenge. And feeling great really comes from the inside out. No, you don't have to compete with others and show everyone how much happier you are than them, that's not real happiness, just bragging a bit too loud perhaps. Having meditated for decades, done many types of body work, reiki energy healing, visualization techniques, yoga, weight lifting, running, aikido, Tai Chi, aerobics, Tantra groups, therapeutic transformation groups, sound healing...and more...

> *"The problem with people, is that they don't know enough about feeling good."*
>
> *Richard Bandler* [1]

...acupuncture, stone healing...therapeutic dance...Feldenkreis (movement integration)...pretty much most kinds of exploration of feeling and therapies. It's all the same somehow, and grows over time. If you get a chance to be around people who have mastered their emotional states and expanded and amplified their energy, being with them and learning from them can be a springboard to the "happiness habit." And emotional wellness is considered an important contributor to physical health. Now that this is highlighted and noted, let's cut to the precision goal setting, so please grab a pen.

> Precision direction-
> Step One-
>
> Write down something or a few things that you really want or have given up on, and something you would like that you never thought of before.

New thoughts and desires

*

_____

_____

_____

_____

_____

_____

_____

_____

_____

_____

_____

_____

_____

Step 2

Take the most enticing one from step one and write a paragraph or few sentences about the feelings that having this in your' life is or would be like. Make sure this is something that you really want or feel drawn toward deeply, or find something else. Please think about this first, and write concisely.

_____

_____

_____

_____

_____

_____

Step 3-Make a picture or hear what it would sound like *having* what you want *now*. See, hear and feel...whatever it is. *Amplify* the *feelings* and everything, *step into* the picture as if you have it, hear what you will hear, make it surround sound and cinamax... *bigger now*...twirl feelings inside...let them grow. Make it real life in all senses, and even bigger NOW...that's right! Let those experiences come up and grow every time you even do something infinitesimal towards them, such as seeing your' future, taking care of little things and even smiling.

```
Step 4


Write what won't
happen when you
totally and absolutely
get what you want.
```

_____

_____

_____

_____

_____

_____

Step 5

Write what will
happen if you don't get
what you want.

_____

_____

_____

_____

_____

_____

_____

_____

```
┌─────────────────────────────┐
│          Step 6             │
│                             │
│                             │
│     What won't happen if    │
│   you don't get what you    │
│           want?             │
│                             │
└─────────────────────────────┘
```

_____

_____

_____

_____

_____

_____

Now, putting your new vision and direction for something that you truly desire in place and in your' future with clarity and strength will set in motion a process of focus and self realization of the desires and wants. Yet, you may discover something even deeper, perhaps a longing for something higher or you can call it deeper. No one can tell you your' deeper meanings or purpose, that can be discovered by you only. And if you see or feel something that moves you deeply, please give that energy and space in your' life. Disciplining the subtle things in life seems paradoxical. Yet, if you recognize something inside yourself, that perhaps you had forgotten, don't forget to remember them. Making time in your daily or weekly activities for activity or non-activity that nourishes deep feelings that you have about or for something in your life, can only expand and attract the things you are longing for on a deeper level!

Having something that drives or pulls you forward is what Victor Frankel[2], the Austrian Psychiatrist, spoke about in his book, "Man's Search for Meaning." He thought that having a compelling future or meaning helped him survive the concentration camps in Germany. His desire to be able to live to tell about his experience to prevent such a horrible thing from happening again helped him get through. To me, this is a poignant example of how having a compelling future, one that pulls or drives the emotions, can help create energy that propels a person with vigor and fortitude.

Adding precision direction exercises are the same as making space in your' daily or weekly activities to nourish something you really want. In that, when you step into your dreams the thought of having them alone, make the chances for them happening, even more. Such is the way of attracting what you want. One of the tenants of healing or transforming something is to "let go." This principle works on different levels for small and larger things and applies to attracting and manifesting too. Just like when we have to be able to let go to be able to change something as opposed to holding on to unhealthy thoughts and feelings. So too, do we need to notice what we really want, and strive for that. Being fearless and going for what you know you truly want, instead of being stuck can be done with precision and intricacy. Now, what does it mean to be the master of our minds?

1. Bandler, Richard, Master Practitioner live quote (Button), Beverly Hills, CA, June, 1999

2. Frankl, Victor, *Man's Search For Meaning*, Beacon Press, 2006

10-Don't Draw Conclusions

Your mind is there to serve you, and you are not your mind. But if your mind is using you then just remember, you are not your thoughts but something more than that. To define what the mind is, is probably different to many people.

If you look at someone who seems calm and tranquil, you would probably agree that they have a calm mind. Yet, how can someone have a calm mind in difficult circumstances? Ultimately, most people, if not all people have times where they seem like the overwhelm is permanent and will not go away. Or even worse, they are overwhelmed and are not even aware that they have the power to learn to be the one at the controls or feel certain they are powerless. Yes, they are actually the one running their own brain! In fact, no one can run your' thoughts except you ultimately. Yet our brains don't come with owner's manuals, we have to learn how to use them via trial and error as well as conscious effort and awareness. And some good news is that lots of effort has been made to understand people's internal processes recently, which makes recent times very potent for individual understanding and discovery. The good news is that, certain patterns of thinking give good and effective results. Once you discover some of these, it seems easy.

If you think of an experience that you have had that was really good. And notice where you were in that experience. Then step into it, see what you saw then, hear what you heard, and feel what you felt. Now notice the image you have in your mind of the experience. Make it bigger and turn up the sounds, make it life like...like you are actually there now. Your' feelings probably magnified and expanded when you made the images bigger, didn't they. Now, make it more bright and zip it bigger. This is the same process people use to feel overwhelm, except they are blowing things out of proportion that aren't positive thoughts. Sometimes one way of getting resolution to a complaint you feel like filing or bringing up regarding anything, is not to file the complaint. Stop noticing it, or diminish it so it is nonexistent now. You may notice that your' continued focus and bringing it up and thinking about it would make your feelings loop in a negative direction or way. And the inverse is true too. Positive feelings inside associate with positive images and effect each other in a positive loop or direction and location in the body.

So, just as your' body needs time to recuperate from stresses, so too does the head. And depending on how you have treated and used your' body will determine how much time is required. So, it is the same for mental stress in a way. I am not trying to make an exact comparison, nor do I want to. The important point is that sometimes there may be times when you are so overwhelmed and don't "see the light at the end of the tunnel," and you just need time to recuperate. And there is an opposite of this kind of; sometimes you need time to recuperate, when you don't even know that you are overwhelmed. Just as we can de-tox our bodies, so too can we sort of de-tox our minds...really! And when you do that cleanse, or get away for a while or get in tune and feel your destiny or whatever moves you, you may laugh and say, "why did I wait so long." It is sometimes hard to get perspective when we are in the "muck." That is why it is funny looking back on those times sometimes, because that is new perspective. It is normal to deal with stress. I was recalling how many different times I have moved into new places, reflecting on the past as I have traveled quite a lot having lived in a few different countries and also visiting many different countries. I remember one time moving back to the Puget Sound Islands from Japan in the late nineties, and I just couldn't relax and was totally overwhelmed for several days. I was pressuring myself to control my mind and relax, but I couldn't. I think this added to the stress level. Plus, I felt frustrated because I had studied relaxation techniques and Yoga in India, centering oneself with martial arts in Japan and had learned much about the subtleties of thoughts and feelings doing lots of trainings with successful therapists and Psychologists all over the world. The time change of fourteen hours and sudden cold did not help either. Also, going from facilitating an intense ten day certification training in a totally modern city taking subways every day to being in the woods with a bunch of hippies was quite a contrast. In speaking about this experience, a few years later, to a friend who is a Native Healer there on the island, he told me about some of the Native Saseewa People's experiences during something like a vision quest, saying my descriptions sounded similar.

I wanted to share this not so much as an example of how applying the healing ways can change things like overwhelm and fear. But as a reminder that even when the world comes apart at the seams, sometimes it just takes a little time...or perhaps just going on a long drive. And why freak out? That just makes it worse. Just because you don't know how to change something shouldn't be a cause for alarm. Remember, sometimes it is imperative not to draw conclusions. Or if things aren't changing fast enough, be a little patient. Fast changes will come in their own time, being impatient for quick change is great and works. Yet, if the impatience seems to create more stressors, do something else.

Sometimes the mind wants to draw a conclusion. And sometimes there is no way to really understand what is happening in the moment. Drawing conclusions too fast can limit what a person is experiencing. This can happen in two ways. Making early conclusions regarding inner experiences can limit the awareness to new information. And it can create stress by perpetuating the need or desire to find an answer. This perpetuation or fear to understand the unknown is a limitation in that fear breeding fear only creates less understanding, not more clarity. Clarity is subtle, and needs patience sometimes. Which brings us to the next way to heal...meditate.

11-Alter Your' States

One time I was having lunch waiting for a connection to go to the beaches on the Sea of Arabia in Goa, India. I ran into an old friend from India there and we were talking about the differences of the West compared to the East, and also how India had changed over the last twenty years or so. As such conversations go; it seems that the past seems to be truer or richer of experience. He being from India, the oldest culture, and myself from N. American culture, the youngest, can bring up interesting contrasts.

We were sharing about the cool dance parties we used to go to in the early and mid 90's, and sort of bragging to a few other people how great it used to be. And a lot of us used to go to meditation retreats where you may take several days and some people even months or years and just meditate in silence with an experienced teacher or guide. Or meditate with many others for an hour or two each day in silence. And I was commenting on my enlightened experience of learning this one teachers meditations, who was quite well known there. And my friend, Ameen, said, "did he say that?" As, I had said that of the many words he had said, all he said to do was "just meditate." And I thought about it and had to say "no." This famous meditation teacher never said to meditate...yet that is what he teaches more or less. Every day all year long, they make available certain meditations at certain times, but never once did the Meditation Leader say, meditate. I guess he was preaching by example because the environment that was created there made it easy to meditate. To a typical western person, meditation may seem like something strange but it really is just about developing subtle awareness, not concentration or disciplining one's mind per se.

Now some people even say that simple things are meditation. In Japan, the Japanese Tea Ceremony is considered a kind of meditation and so is Kendo or sword practice. I do not know about you, but seeing someone with a black belt on, take out a Three and a half foot long sharpened sword with Kanji Characters etched into its metal, and hearing the resonating, "zzhing," as it comes out, makes me pay attention to what is going on. Now, there are many kinds of meditation, Zen, Vipassana, Chakra Breath, Nadabhrama, Kundalini, silent, humming, chanting, mantra's, more active meditation's and guided visualizations to name a few. But to me, learning to alter my own state by going into trance and doing guided internal relaxations has gotten good results of increased clarity and increased life satisfaction. Taking time to explore all the parameters can be beneficial and can increase awareness all the way around. Someone told me once, "If you could jump into another person's body, it would make LSD look trivial," since we all have such unique worlds and points of view that we live in. People are actually going into different kinds of trances and meditative states all the time...driving trances, at work trances, learning trances, so many different states of being. In fact we still don't know how we can understand language, that is, it has its own "trance" state, I guess you could say. So, exploring and experimenting with altering your' own state of being leads to better understanding of yourself and the limitless possibilities that people have inside themselves. But Deepak Chopra, an esteemed Doctor from San Diego offers free online 21 day meditation challenges, you can subscribe to the Chopra Well, all explanations are given there, and you can be part and connected with a larger group of people who are into a "consciousness awakening" activity. It is done very simply, concisely and in a heart full way led by Dr. Chopra and his trainers.

Learning to quiet internal dialog and stop the mind can be calming. This is one of those things that once experienced is like getting a new lease on life, but is free to do. You do not need a TV or any subscription or even a cable connection. Greater relaxation and calm as well as clarity are inevitable with inner exploration.

Hypnosis is often used as a bridge to meditation or vice versa. Calming the mind, going inside and finding tranquility are characteristics of both. If you don't think you can get yourself to relax for any period of time, sign up for a ten day Vipassana retreat where you have to do this in silence. Or you can meditate every day for a year or two, make a commitment. Then you will almost certainly have this relaxation skill forever. Going into silence seems to work...yah...yes sometimes you may just want to stop all internal dialog on the inside too, not just silencing the outside talk! Did you ever have one of those times where you encountered someone who you really did not want to deal with because they talked too much and you just wanted to tell them to shut up, or you just had to escape or leave? Well, doing the same thing and quieting your' own internal dialog and stuff can be just as effective for your' own development and inner calm sometimes.

If you can find someone who is a master at hypnosis, you can probably experiment with listening to CD's or MP 3's...notice if you feel more relaxed. Changing your' point of view for brief or short moments using tools like hypnosis or other relaxation techniques can open new doors for new decisions and more healthful behaviors and life styles. Use this as a tool and remember that you can go to deeper levels, just like peeling an onion. It is not about where you are in time, but when you are in time...time is relative to our perspective because sometimes it goes by faster or slower. But time doesn't change, we change in those moments. Developing these habits can alter this. These habits should feel rejuvenating and that is what they are for on a healing level especially. If you meditate with someone who has done lots of meditation, it should be easier and a transfer can happen that can help a person to get the knack of it in an easy and effortless way, and this should lead to more calm tranquility in all areas of life. If you meet a meditation teacher that you feel attracted to, that should be a criteria.

The element of knowing oneself also plays into the meditation game. When you quiet down inside, you come closer to your' essence. In my experience, lots of love and joy come out meditation. It's like you can become available to a whole new experience. If life is a gift that is a joy for no reason at all, meditation can reveal the gift. This can seem very simple or very complicated, and seem never ending. And eventually, it is a tool that doesn't need to be practiced. So, really, this is just a development of awareness somehow. First person point of view is seeing life through your' own eyes. Second person point of view is seeing from the others person's eyes. Third person is seeing both people from the middle point. And fourth person point of view is seeing both people's point of view at the same time. Meditation and trance is going inside and exploring and feeling and just witnessing, noticing what is going on. It is defined as going from your' current state, whatever that is, to a different one. Sometimes it is mind blowing, don't draw conclusions too soon. Some just start by watching your' breath, mind or emotions...this exercise on awareness can create new experiences. Watching your' breath can be done. Then a person can move on to even more subtleties like noticing and observing the mind or even finer are the observations over time of emotions. If you find yourself being a "practicer" of mediation in a daily practice, I would say to just remember to try to "be meditation." You can prepare meals in a meditative way, drive meditatively and even walk meditatively. And some of the systems that we learn as we grow up that no longer serve us are perhaps some of the very things we need to unlearn. Taking time and making our own conscious directions for the finer things in life each time and every day can be attained in meditation. I do not claim to be a meditation teacher, just a person who experienced meditation, and I am still learning and experiencing. I like the immersion method, where you may immerse into a meditation group as opposed to just doing it on your own. Please remember, if you do an immersion, plan on needing at least a few days or a week to come back to the "real" world. Also, Vipassana Meditation is great yet was designed around 2,500 years ago and there are newer kinds of transformation and tools available. Yet, the 21 day meditation challenge online, was very gratifying as it is being done by thousands of others, so you feel part of something bigger. They are teaching meditation to inner city kids in the Bronx, New York as an alternative to usual inner city life. And the music and guides are very nurturing and supportive, and you do not need any time for reintegrating into the normal world, so it is quite easy. Having done many different kinds of meditation and inner exploring I even suggest Deepak's 21 day meditation challenge to all my friends because I believe it can be personally transformative as well as socially transformative. Can you think of a better time than now to bring more calm and clarity to the world?

12-Scramble Pattern

Scrambling unpleasant experiences gives them a chance to be re-scripted and re-coded and it frees up wasted energy for better things like feeling pleasure or whatever you want in your' life. Now, if you do not have anything unpleasant that you want to forget about or lesson the nagging these habitual memories can conjure up, then great! You may have someone that you know who you might share this with. Yet, if you do have something that seems to bother you and you would like to change it, the scramble pattern can scramble it so it does not have a grip on you or your' thoughts anymore. Or if you are a person who just likes to experiment with new mind sets, you can test this with your' own feelings and internal skill sets. The first time I did this I wanted to get rid of a feeling I would get when I thought about what a certain person had said to me one time. The feeling I had was one of lack and self doubt. Even seeing the person or thinking about this person perpetuated the feeling, even though they were not treating me the same way as that one time where they said that one thing in a certain way to me, that had initially started this emotional pattern. Now, in doing this scramble pattern, literally in 5 minutes, the feeling changed forever all the way until now. These patterns were created by the co-creator of Neuro Linguistic Programming or NLPtm, Dr. Richard Bandler, by studying several people who had had a phobia of certain things and had gotten over it. And this was found to be effective for phobic feelings and even traumatic or strong ones.

The pattern shown below is useful for nagging memories or feelings or one time events that seem to have generalized into larger realms. Also, this is effective for feelings or events that were traumatic. Traumas are very difficult and fragile to work with. One reason is that people do not like to think about them, after all, they were traumatic. But through a process called disassociation, the emotion can be separated and looked at from a different point of view, therefore, giving a chance to recollect and healthfully re-script the associated memories without overwhelm diminishing unwanted feeling. Since this is a visualization and series of internal visual sequences, having a quiet place to do this in the first time can help but is not mandatory as long as you are not distracted and do the whole process about five times.

So, the first part is to imagine you are at a movie theater and waiting for the movie to begin. Now as you notice yourself sitting there, float up and watch yourself waiting to see the movie which is about to begin shortly. Now just float up into the projection booth...where you can look down and watch yourself sitting there looking at the screen. Now hit the start button on the projector. You are watching yourself, watch the movie screen. Now being there in the projection booth, start the movie from just a little bit before the very first unpleasant experience...see yourself in black and white first, but watch yourself sitting down there from the projection booth, watching yourself watch that B&W movie that you are in. Make sure you can see yourself...watching yourself on the screen. Play the movie all the way through until the end...still watching your' self watch that movie. When it gets to the end, make the whole thing white, flash it white...and white it out as if the movie reel ended and the whole screen is white. Now, hit the reverse button and watch the whole thing backwards...make sure to step right into it and associate to it in backward mode...that's right...everything going in reverse.................................now...sounds...every-thing...moving backwards...in color now...hear the backwards sounds and see everything first hand in re-wind mode...when it gets back to the beginning...white it out again. Now, play it forward again watching yourself down there watching the movie........................all the way toward the end of that experience then white it out again and then reverse it...step into it again, seeing everything going in reverse, in color this time and hearing it all in reverse coming back toward the beginning then white out the whole thing again..vooosh...white it out!!!!! Now this time when you watch it again in black and white add some circus music....watching yourself watch... da duh da duh da da da duh duh da da da.........................going all the way toward the ending then vhhhooooosh...white it out and rewind it except in fast mode this time then whiting it out at the beginning again...VOOOOSSH! Do this at least a few more times each time making it more ridiculous perhaps adding Disney Characters like Mickey Mouse and whiting it out at the end and beginnings until you will notice that whole event has changed into something quite different.

Now, when you think about the old memory it should be scrambled and a different set of feelings and associations will be available to at a minimum flatten the old or perhaps even instill curiosity or humor. See yourself in a future similar situation and notice how the feelings are different, aren't they? Representing a memory backwards will recode the meaning as well as interrupt the old unconscious patterning of memories and take away the nag or hooks and in turn free up new feeling and meanings.

Make sure that you see yourself in the movie and don't see the movie from your own eyes or point of view and step into the movie when running it backwards. That is the difference between seeing an experience from your own eyes or seeing yourself in the experience. This distinction in perception of seeing a memory of an experience through first person point of view versus seeing yourself in the experience is called disassociation. Association to remembered experience or disassociating to the experience can have a significant effect on the feeling attached to certain memories and is an important healing perceptual tool and skill. Running it backwards enhances the "let go" even more and re-patterns things. This mode of disassociating while seeing and visualizing is called a visual sub-modality. In this case, seeing yourself over there on the screen or in the picture, or seeing the picture from your' own eyes, like it is happening right in front of you.

Now, we could go back and analyze your' past trying to find out the underlying meaning to these traumatic events. Or we could do this exercise and I would not even have to know any detail about what happened to you. All I would need to know is that you have some feeling or memory that nags you, that you want to get rid of or interrupt or change. In turn, this is content free, where the content does not have to be analyzed or shared with anyone. And changing *how* a person represents things inside themselves is first priority, not understanding why or what they are representing in their mind as such.

So, the scramble pattern is included here because it embodies many of the other ways to heal all in one little visualization. No, it is not intended as a cure all, but is intended to do what it does, scramble nagging, disempowering stuff! It can facilitate in letting go, enhance peacefulness, create inner awareness and add to self sanctity. And this is a practical common sense worldly tool. And being objective about our internal processes and not so identified with them, taking a step back, increases intelligence and clarity of mind as well as confidence in how to "run" and use your' own brain and thoughts with easy and articulateness.

13-Enhancing Positive States

Internal Pharmacy

If you have ever had the experience of having a natural high after doing something, this is what this is about. Maybe you had just been out sailing or doing a cruise on water, or perhaps had just seen or heard a great show or concert. Those feelings you have inside yourself from these kind of experiences can begin to come into your' life now with your' own volition, instead of just letting your' consciousness wave and flow in the wind. Now that does not mean that you don't need to see concerts or go sailing anymore, that's not the point. We can direct our own internal processes in a way that gives us better feelings, what are called positive emotional states. We all have rich resources and experiences inside us. And in these positive states, life can grow and flow the way we make and create them conciously. And in an easy way, that requires less stress and can be quite effortless. Whatever word you want to call them, learning to effect your' own physiology and states is real and whatever your mind imagines is remembered by your brain and in turn effects your' body and physiology. Now, what you imagine, hear and feel inside isn't what's most important, but *how* your' doing these things is. The awareness that builds from being aware of "how" we do what we do inside ourselves is where expansion and will power can really grow, as well as the skill of letting go and clearing our own minds with volition and ease. If you are hanging around people who habitually live in bad feeling states, you will notice that being around people who feel good is infectious. And consciously taking time to develop the awareness, positive feeling states bring into your' life, can make this happen on your' own. And when your' feeling good for no reason at all, others will gravitate to you and be attracted to you. This can enhance the little things or mundane things in life to create more juice in life and many believe that the habit and ritual of creating positive emotions and feeling states is an important key to a healthful life. Below is an excerpt of how to consciously change your state. Of course you should notice your feelings and well being enhanced in just a bit of time. If you are doing this with someone else, you may enhance the experience by reading a little slower, and can tune your' senses to notice subtle changes in them such as, change in breathing, skin tone changes, and even voice tone change. Sometimes the voice will get deeper and softer, and you may notice the sound emanating from a new area or location in the other person doing the enhancement. All of these are signs that state enhancement is happening. If you are doing this on your' own that's just fine too.

Now, noticing where you are at, hear and see where it is. While you are sitting or lying there, notice any sounds and let them bring you inside even more and notice something you weren't aware of, like the weight of your feet there. As you turn your attention inside yourself, let any distractions bring you deeper inside even more now.

And a few of those pleasant experiences will be explored and tasted in just a little bit. But before you begin to have a deep experience without any trips, drugs, exercise or whatever you like to do to enhance your mind even more now. Just continue noticing and seeing in just a moment how easy experiencing inside experience is. Flow down a little deeper........feel the weight of your body, and begin to notice your' deeper unconscious now. Have your unconscious now, begin to conjure up and present to you a really desirable feeling state you experienced that you will want and enjoy to experience again and

111

you know bringing that in your' life is beneficial for you in your life.

Remember a time or two when that juicy event happened. Recall that "fungasm" of a time and enter into it...the memory of that time can flow to you or around you even. Now step into the picture or image...hear what you heard and feel what you felt. See this experience through your' own eyes...make it bigger....turn up the sounds and volume...make it surround sound...feel the feelings even stronger now...double the size of the image....zzzziiip...double feelings....nnnnnoooowwwwwww....again.....and ....again! Notice where the feelings are..................the location of the feelings and the direction that the feelings spin in, just allow the feelings to spin even more...and as they do...notice if the pictures are still framed or moving...panoramic or different sizes...and add more brightness..turn up the brightness and color...make it bigger...bring them cloooser and now let the sounds vibrate inside and swirl the feelings and begin to spin them even more...........even adding some more color to them or any pleasing color to them now...allow the spinning feeling to expand even further, a little more now...that's right. And notice where your' good feelings are now and your' feeling pretty good, aren't you? And perhaps you can ask, "what would happen if I used my brain and mind consciously every so often in an easy and effortless way and made these positive feeling states an inherent life happening. Now, take a deep breath and let it out. And slowly come back and notice your' body...taking as much time as need...gathering the learning's and subtle insights.

You can remember these feelings even in unexpected situations, such as when turning the door handle and opening the door when you come home. It's literally that easy sometimes, and bringing positive feeling states into your' life can grow, expand and make their way into your life in delightful and even unexpected ways.

Being a person who takes time to consciously enhance your' own emotions is something that grows in you and in your' life over time and in each person's individual way. And doing this with others is something that can be learned in a predictable, systematic fashion. Awareness expands and grows, just like any other discipline or habit. Using our own internal resources gives us a whole pallet of life experience to draw from and is enriching without having to go anywhere or spend any money. Expanding and enhancing our emotions by using these positive life experiences can affect the patterns we have inside ourselves that set in motion evermore states of clarity, calmness, tranquility, ecstasy, genius, dynamism, true joy and positive actions and decisions. Using our own "internal pharmacy" can not only be fun and enriching, but can change the gestalt of what our internal processes are to us and how they work. And this can create new and different levels of insight, understanding and awareness of life experience and living each and every day. And this is something that can grow over the long term, building a little bit more and more over time without serious disciplined effort. Which brings us to one of the most valued emotional feeling states... gratitude!

14-Healing with Gratitude

Being grateful for life eliminates a lot of the "negative" emotions. And lessoning the amount and number of negative emotions we feel, you would probably agree, is a healthy approach to take. This can be considered a general rule of thumb. When you feel gratitude often, most of the trivial things of life are put aside or diminished. This is, in and of itself, self fulfilling and healing and one of those prized and golden emotions. Despite all of the outside attractions and games of life, just being alive is a gift. Some of the happiest people you will meet are those who have very little or perhaps even next to nothing. I am reminded of this more so in poor countries I have traveled in or lived in. Where a high percentage of people may be living in poverty. Perhaps living on around a dollar per day, yet many of them look really happy, maybe since they have less of a chance to feel bad about being poor, having nothing to compare it to. They have to find the little things in life to make them happy, maybe like seeing someone smile and looking them in the eye. Or waking up and realizing as the sun is up, so too is there another opportunity and another day to experience life. Cultivating gratitude can always start right now, just really realizing and acknowledging how mysterious and full of wonder life is. Being alive, the miracle of life, and the enormity of the universe is fathomless. Breakthroughs in science and technology allow us to take control of our destinies in ways never before. The opportunity to earn money, study nearly anything or everything, and travel, is limitless and expanding. To look at the world and just feel grateful for the wonder of the times and immensity of the universe is easy, and can be truly gratifying.

You can always find something to feel grateful for. And in your deeper moments of gratitude, you may want to relish the moment and savor it, perhaps even make a kind of ceremony to life even, by lighting a candle or sharing a gratifying meal or something special or unique or even holding someone's hand in silence. Some time you may just want to close your eyes and enjoy the internal feeling, feeling that gratefulness for no reason at all. And this type of feeling may even overtake you in moments so much so that they just grow and pulsate and bathe you all over in a way.

And if you are feeling ungrateful or feeling stuck you can ask, "what could I feel grateful for if I wanted to?" And what about that makes you feel grateful? Step into the feeling and notice how that feels, let the feeling expand even more. Feeling grateful attracts more of the same kinds of feelings and experiences into your' life. What you put your energy and attention on tends to manifest even more. Energy flows where your' attention goes. We can use a lot of energy people take of trivial stuff and instead of that, by having gratitude, shift a lot of those things into more positive feeling states of being. After all, life is a gift to be grateful for, not a problem to be solved. I really doubt that one day we will arrive to all the answers in life nor would we want to. Yet, if we approach it as an illustrious gift to be cherished, we will look into the mystery and undiscovered parts of it. Realizing the greatness and vastness of it all, makes it an undiscovered smorgasbord to relish and savor with gratitude. After all, you can't really know what you will find or get next. Life is like a box of chocolates in some ways right? Living with positive expectancy can even attract more wonder and positive directions into life. And you don't have to be poor to be happy, just remember that enjoying the "little things" like seeing a person's face or a smile or even small talking to someone makes for a happy life.

15-Experience Another Culture

If you have ever had the chance to live in another culture, my guess is that you would recommend it to anyone else as a positive experience. Why is living in another culture worthwhile and valuable?

First of all, you have to learn a whole new set of rules and ways of doing things. This in and of itself needs awareness and tenaciousness. It is easy and comfortable to be where you are at, the ideas and ways of thinking that we grew up with were basically given to us through our upbringing and education systems. A lot of places teach and try to give people open mindedness and a well cultured education. But quite frankly, sometimes you need to just jump into something new and immerse yourself to really see a personal change or transformation be it going to another culture or not. Some people really just aren't interested in going to another place and that is fine. That is one of the cool things about America, it has so many different cultures where you can just go down the block and see something new, yet it is a double edged sword. Experiencing new points of views is valuable for personal development and can be true of any kind of change a person wants to talk about or achieve. I guess you could say this is like making a trip to the island of dreams and vowing to never go back...so you burn the boat. Burning the boat makes you fully utilize any resources that you have. Burning the boat makes you even draw more out of yourself and finding hidden resources and abilities that may have been hidden or dormant inside of you and needed some reason to spring up. Setting it up to where you have to take action to where your' survival depends on a higher level creative action, in possibly unknown areas, is where transformation and deeper insights sometimes lay waiting. How does going to another culture effect this process?

Well, this is similar to the chapter getting away for a while, except getting away for a longer period of time and immersing yourself in a new activity be it, scuba diving, learning a language, teaching, taking a massage course, learning local cooking, volunteering for something like the peace core, or just doing an extensive around the world trip and photographing it. Recent brain research has verified that if you take on a new habit such as the ones described above, that the brain actually creates more nerve connections, and stays active and intelligent through a person's whole life. One key to this, is having a new action that you do every day. And just being in a new culture is a new action just like learning a new language is, because a total readjustment is usually required.

Another way that living in another culture is healing, is that it makes you appreciate where you come from and grateful for what you already have. It gives you something to compare to. Now if you do go to another culture and take something from that culture, you can always come back and share what you have learned, and find out that people are pretty much the same and that they are all pretty good especially if given the chance to be. When you strengthen the belief that the world is a pretty good place, from having new experiences, it can make your life better.

Another way that going to another culture is healing is through taking on a new identity and letting others go. When you get away and meet other travelers, and stay where they are staying, you will discover that you are not defined by the country you were born in so much as by what you make of your' life, and who you decide to become. Your conditions and upbringing do not determine who you are so much as who you decide to become and how you create your' life. Getting out and meeting people from all over the world will give you a taste of who you would like to be. As you meet different types of people, you will gather experience and begin to see the characteristics that so many different cultures and societies imbibe. Wouldn't it surprise you to learn that something that seems totally normal to one person is totally strange to another. Many of the things that we hold true are just true because of habituation or cultural conditionings. Now, I am not saying to reject everything from your own culture and take on all the beliefs and habits of another place. Keep them, but just be aware and notice what is going on somewhere else. In doing so, a comparison will happen in your' life and a surprising thing will begin to happen, you will start to consciously become aware of your' collective belief systems and conditionings and habits. Over time awareness will develop, and along with that, unwanted unconscious stuff will fall away. And new more fitting stuff will take its place in your' life that is more suitable to your needs and wants as an individual. It's called growing up, but in a "cultured way." And you will actually have more to give when you go back home. And also, you will realize that "home" is wherever you are.

You may notice a surprising and funny thing if you get the chance to live in different places. It's that people take on the mind set of where they are at. Just like a person may take their behaviors and mind set from work home with them at the end of the day. For example, the school teacher who comes home and wants to be the mentor for their spouse, or the factory worker who approaches activities at home like a robot. Or the classic one is the attorney who cross examines their lover or mate. A parallel exists in different cultures and the unconscious traits that exist in them.

These traits and mind sets that exist in different cultures, especially the subtleties of different cultures minds, is very interesting and an excellent awareness development tool. In the area of trying to be a worldly person and a healer, or a person who is influential, these insights can be gained anywhere, especially through living in another culture. I have noticed that foreign people who live in other lands take on their behavior and communication styles usually unconsciously, that is, they are not even aware of how they are acting. How to get things and compliance in one culture varies. Being aware of different communication styles and patterns of communication is essential to being effective as a transformative communicator. It takes real life experience to notice these things and takes personal change to live and adapt. There is immense value in this burning of the boat and going to another culture. A whole book could be written on this subject, and applied to a healing paradigm of the differences in cultures. Psychology is already noticing this and writing about them, especially the differences between Asian Cultures and Western ones. The upbringings we have that are very much influenced by our religious customs are very evident in contrasts between the East and West. In the East the inner world has been given more relevance through customs like meditation and martial arts like Tai Chi or Karate. Where people use breath and chi energy to create enhanced states of being for the use of certain outcomes. And many of these are for the sole use of personal development. In the West, the non physical has been denied relying on scientific proof as a basis for most everything. The idea that you can stick a few needles at points in your' feet to relieve pain somewhere else in the body seems ludicrous to many western doctors. Now, these types of treatments are gaining more scientific validity. The west values outside rewards and accomplishments and the East has searched the inner. Now western science has discovered what Yogi's discovered over 4,000 years ago, matter is illusory. The creator of Yoga, Patangali, wrote about this. Now Western Quantum Physics has discovered that everything has a vibration and frequency. And that actually even physical objects are vibrating and pulsing with energy. So, you may decide to include exploring what the Eastern Mediators' discovered as a new habit to start if you like when you decide to live in a foreign culture for 1 to 6 months at least, and possibly for 2 to 5 years would really allow for acquisition of a new language, which is known to increase intelligence. So, if you are searching for something and are not sure what or where to find it, maybe going to another culture can nurture something new in you. There are many ways to find some inner peace. And personal growth is perhaps nearing the jet age. Real changes can be made by anyone, easily and faster than you may have ever thought, and in several different ways.

16-This Too Shall Pass-

Transcending Generalizations

If you have ever had one of those times where you were stuck in the muck and "problemed", it seemed like everything would be permanent, and that the problem was pervasive everywhere around you and that you were at fault personally. Well, perhaps you were at fault and you need to learn from that and let it go. But no problem is permanent, and no single problem can have pervasive control over your' life. Why? Because the only way and means a problem can have this kind of control over a person is by the person to allow it to have the control in the first place. Ultimately, we are the one's running our own brains, bodies, nervous systems and thoughts. No one can make you free. If you are not doing that then this is what applying the 20 Ways is about. How to develop healthy and healing patterns that enhance the brain and mind in an easy and enticing way. So, how can people stay stuck? Part of the "stuckness" is habitual internal patterns, part of it is secondary gain investments, in having a certain problem, and another part is lack of awareness of internal processing and how to run your' own brain. And sometimes people are too afraid to leave or change environments, the fear of the unknown is stronger than the pain of staying where they are. Our habitual thinking patterns effect how our brain works and vice-versa even, it's wired around this and how we habitually use our bodies. And yes, science has very recently proven that we can re-wire our brains. So are we just at the mercy of our brain patterns? Does the brain create its own patterns that affect the mind or does the mind affect the brain? The good news is that we can influence and rewire our brains. Science has recently proven that our brains are neuroplastic and can demonstrate neuroplasticity. They are capable of changing and adapting, and do not just automatically atrophy as we get old. So, what the Yogi's discovered over 4,000 years ago, is again being proven by western science; with mind awareness, exercises and meditation we can transform and heal our lives. And using these awareness building exercises and technology this can be done easily and effortlessly.

Many of the defense mechanisms people commonly use in life, survival mechanisms and aggressive language patterns are un-holistic and perpetuate unhealthy thoughts or perhaps even "mental illness." And those are terrible words and people should never ever be called that. Healing oneself from the residual leftovers of these necessary worldly defense mechanisms and being, apart from them, and a part of them is possible. On one level it's agreeable to say that the general world is "crazy" because in order to function and be successful in many

131

places people have to know how to use sometimes seemingly rather cold hearted un-holistic patterns of communication and defense mechanisms! And yet, many people consider healing circles or healing groups and most of the stuff that go along with that, such as the idea of emotional intelligence, emotional development and feelings workshops to be "crazy." Such is life in a kind of "split" world, at least recently it seems. Hence a lot of, healing methods you will find are considered off the beaten path, since they deal with stuff that is not dealt with in typical settings, such as, emotional development, wholeness, integration and emotional intelligence. But nowadays it seems anything is possible too. There are message therapists who work for large companies in New York that go and give quick massages to staff while they are working at their desks, just for the sake of a quick state and energy change. There are care givers in terminal wards giving Reiki (energy healing) sessions as standard protocol in major hospitals in the USA.

Healing is a natural part of life. Getting in tune with our own healing inside ourselves is very possible. In fact, the native Hawaiians' did not have any occurrences of mental illness until the white people came. So in a sense, many refer to mental illness as a white person's disease. I would rather call mental illness and craziness a disease that is a remnant of manipulation and control or resulting from those patterns. Having said this, the place to start here, is building larger general beliefs about what is possible. Having started learning some of the finer insights on how to heal your' mind and take control of your' thoughts presently. Even if you are not sure how you will make it through. Even if you are stuck in the muck and it seems the muddy waters are creeping up on you. First of all this too shall pass. Even though you do not know how, if you can't find the answer, everything changes, this is the only certainty, change will happen. What can be changed and transformed is nearly unimaginable, even though you may not be able to picture that yet.

If you are hurting emotionally, not so much psychologically, we can apply this to that too; this too shall pass. One of the biggest frustrations that comes from problems is not knowing a solution. Sometimes it is just better to get on with your' life, do the things that you enjoy, in spite of the pain or hurt. Realizing in advance that everything will change eventually, can help you get on with what you enjoy. And eventually you find yourself forgetting about what it was that you used to think bothered you, having started more useful and enjoyable patterns of thinking and feeling now. This is how healing happens. That is, doing something you like or enjoy and leaving behind what you don't like and not being stuck in it. Lots of times things just take care of themselves when we just enjoy life and are committed to having a good time no matter what is going on. Pretty soon you find life just flowing along and it's like you are riding on a nice wave and flow of good vibrations that can grow and deepen within each and every day and moment. And when you are out there enjoying, maybe even meeting new people and seeing new things and places, you may laugh at how surprised you are to realize it is easier than you ever thought.

17-The Fed up Pattern

When does healing and change happen? If you take a look around at times where some kind of transformation, change or resolve happened, usually some kind of decision was made to stop the old stuff, or perhaps you were just really motivated to do something new or change something because of a current circumstance or happening. Many times transformation comes out of really positive experiences, ones where you are deeply moved emotionally. This is the realm of healing and this book is a conscious effort to attract, seek out and manifest these positive experiences and they have been highlighted and explored extensively here. But on the level of making changes to habits or grosser things, sometimes "negative" means are used as drivers or motivators. We could be more proactive in consciously getting into the habits and processes' of designing our internal states, and in turn setting into motion chain reactions of choice and conscious creativeness.

All of these can start with a few little or smaller ideas and insights, and these can turn into what we talked about earlier, generative change. Which over longer periods of time, they can set in motion automatic processes and positive, infectious patterns of health and well being. Now, getting ourselves to do the things that we know would be good for us can be called a breakthrough, especially when we feel positive feeling states toward the idea of indulging in new habits, behaviors and lifestyles. But, the area of life, where we are unsure what would be good for us and what can make our lives better, healthier and more healed, is not static and is less definable. The finer subtleties and distinctions of healing and transformation, are many times, just setting in motion new thoughts and feelings and accessing and enhancing what is already inside of you, and amplifying those positive states. Doing this with technique, precision and vision, is what we are doing here.

Now, which kind of these "positive feeling states" are worth enhancing and amplifying specifically? Any that can create relaxation, well being and tranquility, along with physical and emotional vitality. If you have ever gone on the water for some kind of a trip and just enjoyed being there and felt wonderful, for example. Or perhaps you have taken a long hike where you had panoramic views in nature and felt deep tranquility and clarity at the end when it was over. Perhaps you were sharing some unique experiences with family or friends in a unique time or place. Maybe you were traveling in a totally new place seeing beautiful new sights or just relaxing on a beach or in the woods somewhere. Those kinds of experiences and lots of others are already there. It doesn't matter when they happened. You can call the feelings that come from these types of experiences and are associated with them whatever you like, the names are not so important here. Think of times like those and review those and label them with whatever names you would like to give each separate one of them. Each experience probably carries a unique set of feelings that took place when they occurred. And some of the really good feelings people have, came from many different layers and types of experiences. Many experiences carry a whole gamut of positive resources and feelings that when remembered and given energy to, continue to expand and increase the same kinds of emotions and feelings easily. So, you can have several different kinds of emotional states that have different personal experiences associated to, that you would like to draw from and re-experience later through creative visualization and self exploration. For example, ecstasy, tranquility, excitement, relaxation, and so on. You can label them however you want and give them letters from the alphabet at your' liking..."A,B,C", etc. This helps if you ever want to test them with another person by going into one of the experiences and having the other guess which one it is, not by the name of the emotion or experience but by the letter. This is a good way to develop subtle sensory acuity to other things in other people like their muscle relaxation or breathing or the changing pressure in the forehead area of the other person as they re-associate themselves back into different experiences, emotions and events. So if you were feeling serendipity in one recalled experience, you can label that emotion "C," or whatever: perhaps you felt that emotion we'll call "C" in the second, fourth and fifth experience or recalled event. Re-experience all those situations again, seeing what you saw, hearing what you heard and feeling what you felt and coming up with at least four if not more

139

emotions and giving a letter to the names of the emotions that you experienced, makes them easier to label and remember. We all have had many wonderful times and felt many really good emotions in our lives, and knowing how to draw from those only expands them and can be a systematic way to begin new enhancing processes. When you are in one of those states, you don't need to tell people, they will easily be able to see it on your' face or catch your' feeling.

But first, how can we motivate ourselves to do the things that we already know we "should" do? Expanding our emotional intelligence and starting to do this in a systematic way can lead to generative results. But getting ourselves to do the simple obvious little things or sometimes even big things usually takes guts or some kind of larger decision or resolve. If you talk to people who have made these kind of big changes usually they will say that they made a real decision. They just knew that there was no going back to the old patterns once the decision was made. How can we get ourselves to make these types of resolving decisions? One way for real decisions to solidify is to see how the current things that you would like to change but haven't, if keeping their current direction over a longer period of time, will produce less than desirable results, or pain. And instead, see how new behaviors or actions will create resolve and deeper pleasure. This is a decision strategy for making resolving decisions about obvious habits we know we should change but haven't. If you ask, "what was a time where I knew I needed to change something, but I didn't?" And then think of similar situations, at least 3 to 5 different times where you knew that you should change something or were close to making a change or you wanted to transform something and look at each one of those for a brief period. And then look at the next one, then the next one, noticing all those times you really felt like you should change something and do the process again. Seeing the first situation where you really knew that you wanted to make a change but didn't, seeing what you saw then, hearing what you heard and feeling what you felt, and let the feelings build and imagine yourself 10 years in the future and what you will have missed by not deciding to make that change now. Do this with each of those times where you nearly made the change or were motivated to. See what you saw then, hear what you heard, imagine ten years into the future the pain you will feel by not making the change and acting the same way and see what you have missed in your' life. And go on doing this with all 3 to 5 memories a few times. And then imagine yourself being toward the end of your' life still not having made the changes, notice all the negative consequences stacked up and the weight of it all. Stop and take a few minutes to do this now. And continue to gain and expand the inner resolve and power letting the feeling circulate even stronger and perhaps just say to yourself, "I can do it, I want to do it, I must do it, I've got to do it and I'VE HAD IT!" And check your feelings to see if you know for sure that there is no going back and if so... celebrate with something unique, even if only for a brief moment with a dance, unique saying or anything. If you get the drift of the process you can expand on this and add to it until you make it work for you to create desired change.

This is a process used by effective change artists or trainers and some successful therapists. Doing it on your' own will build skill. And with practice can evolve into more successful skill sets over time and gets easier as one develops with more familiarity of the process. Plus, visualizing develops and expands as a useful skill the more it is done. If you get the gist of this, that's great. It is just like being fed up. A common example of this pattern is when, let's say for example, someone you have known does something that you don't really like but maybe don't think too much about it. Then maybe it happens a few more times piquing your' attention and perhaps you question what is going on, or think about taking evasive action or begin to wonder how to respond to this. Then one of the times a similar thing happens from this person, you just can't take it anymore, and get fed up and have just had enough of that and won't tolerate or accept it anymore. You see all those situations and different occurrences where the undesirable behavior took place, running them all together in series of thoughts, one happening one right after the other, and suddenly your feeling shifts and a new decision is made. This same process can be used for creating decisions in our own lives with our own experiences. Sometimes you can notice situations that may have been or could be hurtful to others. Or you may notice other situations, were you needed to do something and take action because some important person said so, or possibly for a health reason.

Another way or approach to making decisions for changing something that can be effective, is by just taking time to reflect on something that you would like, to like to change. That is, find something that you want, to like, to change. Lots of times we just don't feel like changing something that we know we should. If you can just reflect on something like this, and say, "I just wish I could want to change this." Not knowing how or why or when the change will begin on its own, just being honest that you would like to change something if you could, even if you don't want to change it now or know how to. If change was easy and painless, what would you dare to change? And just put the thought out there without any pressure on yourself, or any time schedule or thought of disciplined action. And do this occasionally sometimes for no reason at all. And sometime you may find that you begin to change in the right moment and in the right time, starting easily, and building on that. Creating small successes, that grow over little bits and pieces of time, create resolve and success you are unwilling to turn back on. And once you have made the change for a little while, it gets easier to keep it, leading to more resolve and confidence in the changes you've made over more bits of time. And so the groundwork is set, for making real and lasting change that you can truly know and feel confident will stay with you from these moments, on into the future. Continue building more positive emotions for yourself and all those you care for and interact with each and every day.   Which brings us to the next healing pattern...amplify your'....?

18-Quantum Feeling Booster-

Making Personal Development Fun

Now, in this chapter we will continue to build on expanding feelings and positive emotional states in a little different way here. While many of the emotions that expand into even better feelings take new courses in our daily lives. You too, can begin to imagine new pieces fitting together to make new meanings. As you read these words and understand in new ways that are useful for you and serve your higher aspirations, you can begin to enjoy even now, the process that you are about to experience called quantum feeling boost. Before we begin, in this process we will take some of those positive feeling states that you have experienced and amplify those feelings precisely, efficiently and with vigor. We will also create triggers that will solidify and pair the emotional feeling states with subtle sliding touches. Now, if you are doing these with a friend or partner the wording is written in a specific sequence and having a certain syntax which enhances and deepens the process, allowing you to read directly from the pages in an easy to follow way. Once familiar with the process, this can be done in as little as 10 minutes on your' own and you can add new experiences to it as you like and this can grow into larger patterns on different levels which can be used in different ways. There is a specific sequence that can be used every time, even though the experiences and emotions can vary from person to person and moment to moment.

Firstly, recall one of the positive experiences that we labeled with letters in the last chapter, we will use four or five of these. Second, re-associate yourself in a relaxed way to one of them by seeing what you saw during the original experience, and hearing what you heard, almost like stepping right back into that time and feeling what you felt. Third, enhance the experience by changing the internal subtleties, make the pictures life like and larger, turn up the volume inside and spin the feelings even more and larger, perhaps add more color to it. Fourth, when you are certain the positive state is amplified and not until then or while it is just peaking or about peaking, put your left arm out and extend your' hand out, palm down so *your' hand is floating there in the air*, taking your' other hand or right pointer finger and sliding that finger from your left pointer finger knuckle, in a straight line, toward the wrist. Let the feeling and positive state enhance even more as you slide it. And you can stop and do it again from the knuckle each time enhancing it a little more each time, perhaps saying in someone else's nice sexy voice, "make it deeper" or "enhance it a little more" Anything you like is okay, just expanding and making it more each time, perhaps even doubling it again and again. If you are doing this together with another person let the other person do the sliding touch on the knuckles, make sure you time it just as you notice that

149

emotional state of being, being enhanced. You may notice the person looks noticeably more calm, and their face seems to glow from the inside out, that means the feelings are being amplified. The fifth step to break the state for ten or fifteen seconds by standing up, or taking a deep breath, changing your' thoughts for a few seconds or something. The next step is the previous five steps repeated with different emotional states that you also can refer with letters. It is not essential to refer to the states by letters. But it can, if you are doing this with a person, give anonymity to your' personal experiences plus add interest to the experience. And it is useful if you or someone else is testing it to try and guess which state you are going into just by watching each and every time.

Use the middle finger knuckle for the second experience, and then ring finger building up and getting ready for the quantum feeling boost. And then use the pinkie knuckle for the next one, taking careful attention to make sure the sliding touches are happening just as the emotions are building up and each experience is just nearing total intensification. Now once you have remembered and taken time to recall those four positive feeling states (or more) and allowed them to expand while applying a sliding touch to different places on the back of the hand from each knuckle towards the wrist for each one making them grow and expand even more do the last step.

The final step is to take a few deep breaths, sit back, close your' eyes, go deep inside, allow your' hand to float up in to the air again at just the right time, and have all four or more of the sliding touches applied in exactly the same way all at the same time together now, having the positive experience from all four of those melt and mingle and integrate inside of you. Now, fire off all four of the sliding knuckle triggers, A,B,C and D, together again now, and continue to allow the expansion and integration inside yourself, allowing the learning's to grow and positive feelings to keep swelling up inside, perhaps even saying something on the inside in a sweet and lovely voice, allowing it to resonate and pulsate in and throughout your body. And firing the four physical sliding touches even a little bit further and one more time now, just allowing the integration to deepen even more now and perhaps in a subtly sumptuous way. Just taking a few minutes and as much time as you need to take those positive feelings and experinces slowly come back to now. Just allowing all the learning's and positive feelings you have to emanate and expand for you in just the right way now. Perhaps noticing your' breathing and just allowing yourself the time you need before you open your eyes, feeling refreshed, relaxed and rejuvenated.

So, this is one of the things we do in trainings for people who want to learn and deepen healing skills. This process is very powerful and transformative and only leads to better feelings and life enhancement in all areas. If you can feel good doing even the mundane things like mowing the lawn or driving down the road or going to work or anything, then life becomes a positive flow and the pleasurable and enjoyable things even get better, such is life. This is what happens when we add more inner peace and calm into our lives. When we can effect generative changes, positive things can happen creating quantum changes, adding multiple effects in subtly sumptuous ways. The quiet times can be more quiet, and the exciting and vivacious ones, even more aware, and of limitless possibilities that life has to offer. And taking it all and wrapping it inside, and maybe even saying to yourself, "feeling good can be so easy!"

19-Reverse Conditioning

Now, feeling enhanced feelings and new awareness' helps and makes things easier. It's time to begin to see an enhanced and more emotionally intelligent and perhaps even a more whole and healthy person on all levels, even the subtle ones, since you've started the enhancement, haven't you? Begin to conjure up a picture of this, ultimately enhancing you. This is solely for your own life and for your own purposes. To enhance what you want to enhance in that way you want to. Make that picture of an enhanced you even bigger and enhance it until you feel the intensity of it so that it is distinct and vivid. Now, keeping that in mind, just let the picture of it go into the back or out of your' mind for a little while. With all the visualizations and readings from the last few chapters, along with the emotional state boosts, you should have an ideal image of yourself and a specific one that is unquestionable creatively new if it wasn't already. One that reveals a clearer idea of what you want and who you really are and want to become or have become.

What would happen if you took your' usual self image of yourself and made that automatically remind you of this clear picture, that person that shines from the inside out? When you see the "status quo you," maybe the person you used to be but don't want to be anymore, and instead, see the image of the newer self image, this process is easy and simple. If people have negative self images why not use it to an advantage? You can use the image of where you were, that you aren't one hundred percent happy with, and have the desirable one just replace it automatically inside your' mind. And starting this with great internal feelings, you may notice that your' internal visualization is more lucid, forthcoming and new. Doing this with speed and repetition will automatically "reverse condition" this to where a previous

155

"negative" or ineffective or unwanted thought will be the condition for a new and enhanced thought to emanate from, propel to and exist. So, if you can take the status quo image that you no longer are, and out of one of the bottom corners of it see the compelling picture suddenly zip and replace it even in a bigger size, brightness and stature. Then see the undesired one, and do the same thing again, zip the new one starting out now and make it bigger and more intense size just overtaking the old one and shrinking it. Then white out the whole thought just like the reel coming off or ending on a movie projector and the screen suddenly going white. Do this at least five times, see the undesirable status quo picture, and see the desirable picture come from small size zipping in size to overtake and shrink it. Hear the zzzziiiiip, or make a sssaawwoooooosh sound each time as the pictures change. Make it intense so the feeling change is undeniably noticeable. After having done this reverse conditioning zipping pattern at least five times with uninterrupted speed each time and making the desirable picture and state a little more each time, you should notice that the first thought or image automatically triggers to the newer images, in turn, creating more depth and magnitude which brings more wholeness and healthy feelings and thoughts into your' life in which you created them.

If you like this exercise, you can use it every day for a few months, perhaps in the morning while your' getting ready with progressively enhanced thoughts. Because, getting into a great state is one thing and is a good step. Conditioning a new pattern of emotion over a longer duration on a daily basis can be helpful in furthering these healing ways. And if you can see yourself in the future, perhaps at some planned event or events, carrying new states and traits and having an enhanced demeanor, that's great too! Or you can even see yourself and feel excited or put this feeling into the thought of a unique song now just as a further solidification. So, when you hear that song on the outside or the inside it further solidifies your' enhanced changes into the future. Just

157

because life is really full of surprises and you never know what is next.

20- Word Magic-Healing and changing in Japan

This chapter is a little bit of a diversion in that looking at another country and its language can be used for a metaphor for our own development and how healing and change happen as a whole. In this book, several suggestions and useful ideas and experiences have been presented all in hopes of stimulating new thoughts and in turn outcomes. We will take a look at language and how it manifests in it's culture, perhaps even leading to a better world with lower crime and more peace and even more present oriented-ness.

If you read any books on meditation there is a very good chance that some kind of excitement over Japanese Zen Meditation or Zen Stories will be mentioned. And if you saw the movie, "Caddyshack," Chevy Chase talks of the Zen Poet, Basho, in a humorous way while golfing. And a few friends of mine call their tennis games Zennis, just to bring a different level of awareness and a meditative quality to it. And nowadays, it has become vogue or cool to say something like "Wow that's really Zen." What is so great about Zen that makes Zen famous? After all, many other cultures are primarily Buddhist too, such as Viet Nam, Thailand, and Myanmar (Burma). Zen in Japanese literally means all, total, whole or completeness. Japanese are commonly known for their aesthetic conscientiousness. And when we westerners say something is Zen, we often are referring to an esthetic beauty such as a well organized, decorated room or garden. If you see some of the old style Japanese pottery or Arabeware, it has simple design patterns that are somehow captivating and beautiful, thus being Zenlike. And each piece is unique unto itself. And they even allow meditation in the schools in Japan, it's called meisou, pronounced "may e so oo," a set aside time period to reflect and Meditate in many Public schools. But, if you speak to a person who has studied Zen, you will find a code of speaking that is unique unto itself and has its own characteristics, therefore, carrying a verbal tradition or style along with it and a way of creative expression.

How we speak is very important in healing if you are a massage therapist, a counselor or in any type of human service. And the voice can take time to find and develop and needs to be discovered and still grows over time. Zen people may say, don't say something to its end, leave a space or gap for the listener to partake and respond. The response or interaction is valued or desired. The Zen

Tradition teaches people to understand things that are left unsaid. Implying things is really a part of this culture, and if you do not pay full attention you will not know what someone has said to you or you may understand the words, but miss what is being imparted or implied. If you are just waiting for someone to give you the final answer, you will be lost. Why is this? Part of this is that Japanese language does not have as many verb tenses; in fact very few, so not as many distinctions are made, in language, between past, present and future. So if one really just wants to just "be here now," just stop speaking English or your' native tongue, and move to Japan and speak Japanese! So, the meaning of language in Japanese is very much made and derived from contextual occurrences. And people have to develop their awareness and attention to even understand what is being said. As you develop your' awareness more and more, these kinds of insights will become more inherent. So, living in Japan may automatically develop one's sense of awareness and meditativeness just as a byproduct of the

161

inherent language. So too does being around people who are the masters of language and their own emotional states of being, so you don't need to go to Japan, the resources are inside you and around you. The same thing can happen if you experience silence for an extended period of time. The meanings that words habitually create and the absence of them for a period of time, sometimes open a "window" and a person has a timeless experience. Or in Japanese they say, "Satori," a brief glimpse of enlightenment. Some people talk about going to the desert for forty days and forty nights. And this reveals and reinforces a healing pattern, which is, getting out and having a new perspective on language and words.

And Japan has some very interesting things about that, that people may find interesting. And the people there live longer than any other developed nation; they have one of the highest standards of living, and are one of the most educated and highly literate populous. The children know four alphabets by the fifth grade;

Hiragana, Katakana, Kanji and English, so they are incredibly visual. Yet, if you look at all the devastation they have gone through, they somehow have prospered and used tragedy to grow from and have stayed united and together as a people. And so this is true of what has happened after the Great North Eastern Japan Earthquake of 2011. And they have very low crime rates all around still today, even after becoming very westernized. Right now they are doing studies in developed western countries about how collective mind sets and emotion can influence the greater whole on a collective level.

Words and language are so subtly important and word magic is something that can enhance and expedite any kind of transformation or changing pattern. One thing about change and transformation is that some great energy change can happen to a person, usually on the feeling level, or some kind of break through, but then people sometimes stumble over themselves and get in their own way instead of getting out of their own way and just flowing on a good feeling or positive flow states.

So how to "get out of your' own way" at the right time and place? Sometimes just saying "screw it" or learning to just "stop" any over analysis in certain times, and over time the process get's easier and easier and more awareness is developed on all of the internal processes so you can usually catch yourself. Sometimes when the person who had the transformation gets back and starts talking to themselves and attaching meaning to what has happened to them, many times the old pattern can re-effect the initial transformation. So using positive word magic with yourself can influence very, very subtle energy transformation making them integrative and broaden. So, some initial change happens, that let's say it is real relaxing or transformative for someone, then they start talking to themselves inside and analyzing and sometimes the old pattern comes back, and it can be interrupted too. This does not always happen, but a truly skilled practitioner and agent of change knows how to use words, in a specific way, sometimes seeming magical, to assist other's in integrating new transformations in subtle practical ways. One of which is being able to use language to amplify current resources and transfer them to the future or future pace and test new created states of consciousness into newly imagines scenarios. After all, your' unconscious cannot tell the difference between what it has imagined and what really happened. So in this case, being able to use time words of past, present and future to influence and articulate change adds a whole new level to healing and the integration of new understanding and learning. Using resourcefulness to your' advantage allows people to take the best of what they have in any moment, and allow those kinds of feelings and things to be appropriate in any and every context from the "now" on into the future.

21-Enhancing Rituals

So, this book is about making happen what is being talked about. If you have gained some clarity, peace and a little zest on a feeling level, great!! If not, I would suggest seeking out some people who are experiencing what you desire or wrote about earlier and spend some time with them and find out how they think and why they feel so good. Having traveled quite a bit and seen quite a bit while meeting some of the best therapists and healers has shown me what works. Some ways of doing things just work better than others, being able to recognize the difference is part of this process, as well as practicing and trying new ways of doing stuff inside yourself with a certain attitude of positive expectancy. In light of that, let's take a little look at our daily rituals.

It's the activities in between the times where we spend most of our time that is referred to here. Make space for healthy ritual. What you do after work, after you wake up, at the end of the week, or at the beginning of the week can also be called rituals. When we can take all of these things that have been talked about here and integrate them into our lives in an easy way, those kinds of rituals don't have to be any type of a chore, but more of a relaxation time or a time to just settle down. So some of the rituals that you are already doing that are satisfying for you, may already be set up and set in place in the right way for you. As long as what you are doing works for you...great!! Being able to break un-useful or limiting habits and create better ones always adds more choice, and more choices leads to more freedom in life. And learning new ways to approach life can change reality itself, transforming most everything into something new or different.

Any ritual that can grow, in and of itself, should be considered of greater value, for example, reading or exercising. Some people may have more creative rituals like painting or playing music.

Just the thought of having or bringing some kinds of rituals into your' life can be enhancing no matter what kind of ritual they may be or are. Because being aware of all the different areas of life and how they complement each other can only enhance and add cohesiveness to them if you allow it to. The little things we do are like little bridges that enhance our lives in creative ways, taking us from one place to another and one feeling state to others. If you can add new rituals to your life just as you know that positive and real changes are happening, this is key number one. And after a while you do not have to think about it, you may just have a few rituals that you have grown into lifestyles and keyless doors to a spontaneously satisfying life.

22-New Beginnings

If you are talking about healing such as laying on of hands or spontaneous remission, just believing that you can be healed of whatever is the problem is important. Yet, one thing that is being highlight here, is that the opposite of this is true also. That is, letting go of any rigid mind and belief system can also help healing in order to let something new happen. And more specifically, cutting loose of certain habitual patterns can free up the extra energy that enhances the healing process on all levels.

The healing patterns always try to start with what is desired or the desired state. Why is this an essential part of patterns of success? This is important because energy follows attention, and flows toward whatever you put your awareness on. Then the second step is to notice what is in the way of what is wanted or where you are going to move toward. And, in turn, the differences changed and reconfigured to a new set of thoughts, feelings and results. Manifesting comes from the attention to what is desired, so it is true in healing and well being. So be aware of what you want and put your energy and attention on that.

So one way to add zest to life is having an empowering future, and after getting clear on a few things that really can pull you, these can be external things or more subjective goals like emotional goals, then find out what is preventing you from merging with our empowering future or where you are at now? If you do not have something in your future that inspires you, this is the first thing. Everyone does, yet they may not be aware of it yet. This can range from simple to large. For example, you can feel more alive each day with the excitement and joy of knowing you get to see children grow up. Or you can feel motivation each day that you have a unique insight that no one else has, and the world will be a worse off place without sharing that insight!! Or even simpler, you can feel satisfied every day knowing that, for no reason, life is a joy, just being part of life!

Then you do resource building, which we did quite a bit of here, to find and amplify the resources that you already have. This is a very useful exercise for yourself and others in that it shows us that we all have resources innate in us now, we do not necessarily need anything else added to us. Still, going out and experiencing life and the world and even seeing a new culture could be resource full too. When we enhance ourselves we don't have to have anything wrong with us. And no one is "broken," yet just needs to seek and find new ways for new internal processes to begin and spread throughout their lives.

Healing comes from the new. Ending the old patterns and planting the seeds for what is wanted now and on into future has begun, with new thoughts and determined action. Perhaps you may want to take a vacation, move away, cleanse your body, take charge of your mind in new ways, start a new physical routine, scramble the junky old mind patterns, or just leave or get out of your environment. Ultimately it comes down to your' daily feelings and thoughts and you can quantum boost those in fun ways too, making personal development fun. The quality of your' feelings and emotional states is what determines your' current satisfaction, happiness as well as future manifestations, which in turn, enhances even more satisfaction and so on.

I have found that the best or perhaps the most valuable experiences I have had in life are those that when they ended, were really just beginning. Here is wishing your' positive journey is full of freedom and love and a life that you are proud of. And one that continues to be designed to your' liking on into your' future! ⟫⟫⟫

Suggested Reading

Books

Bandler, Richard, *Get The Life You Want* (Health Communications Inc. 2008)

Wilson, Robert Anton, *Quantum Psychology* (New Falcon Press, 1990).

Websites

Upcoming Training details, online mind tuning as well as schedules are at the Real Changes website.

www.twentywaystoheal.com

www.realchanges.asia